Cookie heaven

Cookie heaven

Hundreds of divine recipes to take you to cookie paradise

DEBORAH GRAY

APPLE

A Quintet Book

First published in the UK in 2012 by
Apple Press
7 Greenland Street
London NW1 0ND
United Kingdom

www.apple-press.com

ISBN: 978-1-84543-460-1
QTT.COO

This book was conceived, designed and produced by
Quintet Publishing Limited
6 Blundell Street
London N7 9BH
United Kingdom

Project Editor: Holly Willsher
Editorial Assistant: Sarah Quinlan
Designer: Rod Teasdale
Photographer: David Murphy
Home Economists: Deborah Gray, Liz Gregory
Art Editors: Zoë White, Jane Laurie
Art Director: Michael Charles
Editorial Director: Donna Gregory
Publisher: Mark Searle

10 9 8 7 6 5 4 3 2 1

Printed in China

CONTENTS

Introduction

Seeping out from the corners of every shopping centre, pavement café and every bakery comes wafting the irresistible aroma of baking butter, sugar, chocolate and vanilla. Cookies, it seems, are everywhere, and now, with the purchase of this book, the aromas from your kitchen can pervade your neighbourhood. The fruits of your labours can fill jars on the worktop, be displayed at garage sales, be donated to parties, wing their way to distant relatives in the mail, all to the delight of cookie fiends everywhere. For is there anyone who can resist a cookie? Cookies seem to appeal to the child in us. They appear sweeter and more intensely flavoured than most cakes, they are crunchy and soft, they are nutty and chocolately, they are easy to handle – they are the perfect comfort food.

Take satisfaction in the knowledge that this book is the only cookie book that you will ever need to own. It contains a unique collection of favourites from all over the world. The word 'cookie' comes from the Dutch 'koekje' meaning 'little cake', and this book contains recipes from Holland as well as France, Italy, Britain, Scandinavia, Eastern Europe and Australia. Every culture, it seems, has its cookies, characterised by the availability of local ingredients and the temperament of its inhabitants. So rustic oaty cookies come from northern Europe, almond-studded biscotti from Italy and delicate, elegant sablés come from France. Then, of course, there are the American cookies. These range from the popular jumbo cookies, stuffed with goodies, to the smaller, simpler cookies, baked straight from the refrigerator.

This comprehensive introduction provides all the background information on the art of cookie baking to turn you into a master of the art. Take time out to read this section before you begin, then return to your kitchen and enjoy yourself. If you have kids at hand rope them in too – they will enjoy the process of baking cookies and it's a good way to have fun with them on wet afternoons. Get them involved in the decorating, especially at holiday times, and your cookies will take on a home-made charm. No kids? Then why not bake with a friend? That way you'll have twice the choice without extra effort, and you'll have lots of laughs in the process. Because after all, you can be really serious about good cookies, but who can deny that part of their charm lies in their frivolity?

The only difficulty lies in the amazing choice this book offers, and the heavenly photographs that make the cookies look so irresistibly tempting. Maybe go for the ever-popular Chocolate Chip Cookies or perhaps the Cranberry and White Chocolate Cookies – eat one with a glass of cold milk to make the perfect snack while browsing through the other recipes to select your next choice.

Be assured that whichever recipe you opt for, the instructions are clearly written and easy to follow, and the ingredients are listed in order of use. With this cookbook as your guide, you can't go wrong.

The Ins and Outs of Cookie Mastery

By simply following the recipe instructions on the following pages you will be able to bake a huge variety of sensational cookies, but it does help to know a little about the equipment and techniques you will be using. You might want your cookies just that little bit larger, chewier or crisper than the recipe suggests, and by understanding the principles of cookie production you will be able to fine-tune your baking to suit your taste.

Tools of the Trade

These are listed roughly in the order of use.

• A set of dry measuring cups, a set of measuring spoons and a liquid measure are all essential. Cooking is chemistry, and in order to get the optimum results, careful attention should be paid to measuring the ingredients accurately. Pour or scoop ingredients into the measures and level with the straight edge of a knife. For butter or other fat, where appropriate, pack down firmly in the measure, then level with a knife.

• A set of mixing bowls, preferably microwave-safe, for melting butter and chocolate in the microwave as well as on top of a saucepan of water.

• A food mixer and/or food processor. A food mixer is great for combining butter and sugar and beating in eggs. It is still best to fold your dry ingredients by hand as it is easy to over-mix in a machine and you risk making the dough tough. A food processor will blend the butter and sugar easily but doesn't result in quite such a light, fluffy mixture as you will get by doing it in a food mixer. However, it is probably preferable to working by hand with a wooden spoon, which can be quite hard on the arms. The food processor is brilliant for chopping and grinding nuts, chopping fruits and for making shortcake and pastry dough.

- A sifter or sieve.
- A wire whisk, or two – one large and one small.
- A grater for grating the zest from citrus fruits and for grating fresh ginger and nutmeg.
- Spoons. A wooden one, plus several teaspoons and tablespoons for mixing and measuring.
- Knives. A sharp pointed knife and a straight knife for levelling are both useful.
- A pastry brush.
- Two or three baking trays and pans. There are a lot out there to choose from. Heavy-gauge aluminium trays are excellent as they conduct heat evenly and swiftly. Nonstick trays are good too, but avoid those that are very dark in colour as they absorb too much heat, which means that cookies may burn more easily. If yours are dark, compensate by cooking your cookies on a sheet of aluminium foil. Insulated baking trays are not as good as they are cracked up to be – they consist of two layers of aluminium separated by a locked-in air space. Cookies do not crisp well on them, and soft cookies spread out too much. If you are using insulated sheets, allow a minute or two extra cooking time and mound cookies generously before cooking.

To maintain optimal air circulation in the oven, cookie sheets should be 10 centimetres shorter and narrower than the oven. For some obscure reason to do with heat circulation, if there are too few cookies placed on a large baking tray, they tend to burn. To avoid this, use a small baking tray or try turning a 20 x 20cm baking pan over and baking on the back. Avoid using tins with edges, since these will prevent good air circulation around the baking cookies.

For baking bar cookies, nonstick 33 x 23cm and 20 x 20cm tins are required. Some recipes also specify other sizes. If you have to use an ovenproof glass baking dish for bar cookies, then be aware that glass retains more heat than metal. Avoid scorched edges and overcooking by reducing the oven temperature by 15°C.
- A metal spatula for removing cookies from the baking tray. Use thin, heatproof plastic if your nonstick surface will be damaged by metal.
- A timer.
- At least two wire cooling racks.

Cookie Types

The ingredients for most cookies are pretty much the same—sugar, butter and a little egg, bound with flour and flavoured with vanilla, spices, chocolate, fruits or nuts. However, the proportions and treatment of these basic ingredients differ, resulting in cookies with various textures and flavours.

Drop Cookies

These are probably the simplest and most versatile type of cookie. They are called drop cookies as the dough is soft enough to drop off the spoon and onto the baking tray. Use the size of spoon recommended in the recipe and encourage the mixture to drop off the spoon by pushing with a second spoon. The basic batter usually consists of butter (or margarine or shortening) and sugar beaten together until light and fluffy. Eggs are then beaten in, followed by flour combined with leavening ingredients and flavourings, either subtle or robust. In addition, textual ingredients are added, the most common of these being oats, coconut, nuts or chocolate chips.

Space the cookies according to the instructions, which will take account of the cooking spread, and bake in a moderate oven. For soft or cakey cookies the mixture should be left well mounded on the baking tray. For a cookie with a deliciously soft, chewy centre and a crisp edge, remove the cookies from the oven as soon as the edges turn golden and while the middles are still soft and paler in color. The more even the colour and the firmer the cookie to touch, the crisper the cookies will be. If you want to make crisper cookies, spread the mixture out a little using the back of the spoon before baking. Some very crisp drop cookies such as Florentines require that the butter and sugar are first melted together to begin the caramelisation prior to baking; others replace some or all of the sugar with syrup. Such cookies generally contain very little flour, which helps them to spread out on the baking tray. Make sure you space these cookies far apart on the tray.

Refrigerator Cookies

The advantage of refrigerator cookies is that the ingredients used to make up the dough can be made in advance and kept in the refrigerator for up to two weeks before being cooked. This encourages cooking on demand so that wonderful fresh cookies can be cooked as and when required without the need to prepare fresh dough each time you want to bake a batch. These are the perfect cookies for those who only have time to prepare food on the weekend, or for anyone who doesn't have the self control necessary to leave half a batch of cookies in storage tins!

The dough for refrigerator cookies is quite stiff, so they are easiest to prepare in the food mixer or food processor. The dough is then moulded into a log or into a thin, oblong brick and wrapped in cling film. Due to their high fat content, the dough must then be well chilled to firm up so that the cookies hold their shape and become crisp when cooked. Slice the cookies according to the instructions given in the recipe using a thin, sharp blade. Space a couple of centimetres apart on the baking tray in a moderate oven. If you decide to increase the thickness of the cookies, decrease the temperature of the oven slightly to ensure that the cookies are crisp throughout. The best way to check that the cookies are done is to sacrifice one and break it in half. Check to see that there is no dark, doughy strip in the centre of the cookie and that the texture is even throughout.

Rolled Cookies

Rolled cookies are the delight of holiday cooks. These tempting cookies can be rolled out and cut into shapes using biscuit cutters, or simply cut into discs using the top of a drinking glass. Rolled cookie dough is similar to that made for refrigerator cookies and often requires refrigerating before rolling and pressing. After chilling, roll the dough on a lightly floured board to a thickness of 3–5mm. Some cooks prefer to roll the dough between two sheets of thick, quality cling film so that the dough can be returned to the refrigerator before cutting. Dip the biscuit cutter into flour before pressing through the dough, then press down firmly to ensure that the dough is cut right through. Gently pull away any scraps, which can be combined and re-rolled. These cookies are cooked in a moderate to moderately hot oven until very slightly golden around the edges and firm to the touch. They tend to be very fragile and need to be removed from the baking sheets after they have cooled for one or two minutes. Use a thin metal spatula or fish slice to transfer the hot cookies to cooling racks. Rolled cookies freeze well for up to one month so they can be made before the holidays and decorated when required.

Pressed Cookies

A plate of delicate pressed cookies always looks fancy but they are simple to make using a biscuit press. They are the perfect cookie for those who would love to make festive cookies, but lack the skill or time to do the fancy decorations.

The dough for pressed cookies needs to be soft enough to be squeezed through a cookie press but firm enough to hold its shape. Extra care must be taken to ensure that the butter and sugar are beaten until really light and fluffy and the flour should be gently folded in by hand. If the mixture is too stiff to press, then add a few drops of milk; if it is too soft, place it in the refrigerator until firm enough to hold its shape. For spritz-type cookies, the dough is generally pressed out onto ungreased, cold baking trays and dredged with coloured sugar or decorated with nuts prior to cooking. To prevent the cookies from spreading and losing their shape, the baking trays are placed in the refrigerator to allow the cookies to firm up before baking in a moderate oven. Remove from the oven and transfer to the cooling racks as for rolled cookies.

Bar Cookies

These cookies fall halfway between a cake and a cookie. They can be thick and chewy, thin and crispy, or light and cakey. Some combine two textures having a crispy outer shell (usually shortcake or crumb based) and a rich, soft topping. Most of these cookies are baked in a moderate to moderately low oven; the cooler oven slows the process of aeration called for in lighter cakes, thus producing a denser and moister bar. For this reason the bars with a crumb or shortbread base often require that the oven temperature be reduced after an initial part-cooking of the base. Always cook bar cookies in the recommended tin. Using a smaller tin will produce thicker cookies, which will need a longer cooking time and will alter the proportions of crust to cake.

As a general rule, these cookies are done when a toothpick inserted into the centre of the pan comes out clean. However, some bar cookies, such as brownies, are best left slightly softer and fudgier than most others. Remove these from the oven as soon as the centre is set and the brownies are just beginning to pull away from the edges of the pan.

Most soft, chewy brownies can be cut with a sharp, serrated knife when cooled. Crisp bar cookies, however, must be cut after 5–10 minutes, before they become firm.

It is also best not to cut bar cookies too big: 8cm squares should be ample – after all, they are supposed to be cookies. Generally, bar cookies keep well if they are left in the baking tin covered with an airtight lid or a piece of foil.

To Market

It goes without saying that good-quality ingredients make the best cookies. However, most of the ingredients required for the cookies in this book can be bought at the supermarket and are not expensive. The most important thing is to make sure that the ingredients are fresh – nuts left over from last Christmas and rock-hard apricots should be replaced, as should spices that have been kept in a warm kitchen in full sunlight.

Flour

Most recipes call for plain flour, which you can buy bleached or unbleached, sifted or unsifted. It is just as well to sift even pre-sifted flour as it settles when left standing. Always sift flour when told to do so by the recipe. Do not substitute cake flour unless stated in the recipe as an option – it contains less gluten and is more powdery than plain flour and will produce a lighter textured cookie. If cake flour is all you have, then, for each cup of flour called for in the recipe, remove 2 tablespoons of flour, then sift well. Likewise, do not use self-raising flour unless specifically mentioned, as this already contains leavening agents and could create dramatic eruptions in the oven if used in conjunction with other leavening agents. Substitute 115g (4oz) of plain flour plus 1½ tablespoons baking powder and a pinch of salt for 115g (4oz) self-raising flour.

Butter

This one is a soul searcher. Butter has an incomparable flavour in baked goods but we all know that butter is high in saturated fat and cholesterol, both of which should be avoided. The problem is that the only substitute is regular, non-diet margarine, and this is in fact not much healthier. The process which turns liquid polyunsaturated oils into the solid fats found in margarine causes the fats to saturate, making them no better than those found naturally in butter. The softer margarines and spreads are healthier but they have a greatly increased liquid content and should not be used in baking unless listed in the ingredients. In some recipes with plenty of other flavours, hard margarine may be substituted for butter although the resulting cookie will be a little softer due to the higher water content of even hard margarine. However, where the butter is absolutely essential for a recipe, such as in Scottish Shortbread, there is really no substitute. Maybe the solution is to make smaller buttery cookies and simply eat fewer of them.

Unsalted butter is best for baking as it allows the cook to fine-tune the salt content of the cookies themselves. Always use unsalted butter when recommended in the recipe. If you only have salted butter to hand, then cut the amount of salt in the recipe by at least half. Salt was originally added to butter as a preservative, so surplus unsalted butter is best kept in the freezer in order to retain its freshness.

Use butter at room temperature when making cookies that need initial beating of butter and sugar, particularly if you are beating by hand because this will cut out some of the hard work. If you need to do this quickly, place the butter on a dish and put it in the microwave on medium and heat for 10–15 seconds (exact timings vary with machines.) In other recipes, where the butter is cut into the flour, very cold butter is essential as the small particles of butter melt while cooking, creating tiny air pockets that result in a characteristic light, crunchy texture.

Sugar

Sugars add flavour and texture as well as sweetness to cookies. Use the type of sugar indicated in the recipe. Brown sugar is white sugar with syrup added to it – treacle in the case of brown sugar, and generally a lighter syrup in conjunction with a little treacle in light brown sugar. Consequently, brown sugar tends to make moister cookies than white sugar. The darker the sugar, the moister and more intense the flavour. Store brown sugar in airtight containers to prevent it from drying out. If brown sugar has already become slightly hard, you can soften it by adding a slice of apple and sealing it up with the sugar in a plastic container for a few days; alternatively, heat it gently in the microwave, checking frequently until softened but not melted.

Many recipes call for granulated sugar or for a finer white sugar, caster. The sugar crystals in caster sugar are very small and will melt much faster than those in granulated sugar, so do not substitute for this.

Vanilla sugar may be asked for, particularly as a decoration. To make vanilla sugar, simply place a vanilla pod or two in a sealed container with a cup or so of sugar. Leave for a week to allow the flavour to infuse; add additional sugar as required and make sure you replace the vanilla pods about once every six months.

Eggs

The eggs used in this book are large unless otherwise specified. It is important to use the correct sized egg or the mixture will be too dry or too wet. Eggs are easier to separate when they are cold but are best used in baking when at room temperature. Very cold eggs tend to curdle the mixture. If you forget to bring eggs up to room temperature, place them in a bowl of warm water for a few minutes. Egg whites should always be used at room temperature to ensure that they whisk to their maximum volume. Always whisk egg whites in a clean bowl that is completely dry and free of grease. If there is even a speck of egg yolk remaining with the white it will not whisk satisfactorily. Start again with a new egg.

Chocolate

The brand of chocolate you select is a matter of taste (and budget); some swear by readily available brands, others purchase special chocolates by mail order. What is not interchangeable is the type of chocolate that you choose. If the recipe calls for plain chocolate, then that is what you should use. Be particularly careful when buying white chocolate chips that you are indeed buying chocolate and not vanilla-flavoured chips. Different chocolates have different quantities of cocoa butter and sugar, therefore altering the chocolate alters the chemistry of the cookie. Always melt chocolate very slowly over a saucepan of gently simmering water or at a medium heat in the microwave (initially for 1 minute, followed by 20-second bursts); either way, remove the chocolate from the heat when it is about half melted and then stir well until the remainder melts and the mixture becomes smooth. Cocoa powder is the pure thing, not cocoa or chocolate drink mixes. Dutch process cocoa powder is probably the best type to use as it has been processed with a small amount of alkali, making it less bitter to taste and darker than its untreated counterpart.

Nuts

It is very important that nuts are as fresh as possible since they do go rancid over time. Buy whole nuts, which keep their flavour longer, and chop them in the food processor or by hand as required. Store in airtight containers – in the refrigerator if you have space. If nuts soften, place them in a 150°C oven for a few minutes to re-crisp. Some recipes call for nuts to be toasted to give a richer flavour. This is best done in an ungreased pan on the stovetop where they can be stirred and watched continuously (they cook very quickly). Otherwise, place them on a baking sheet in a 180°C oven and cook them for about 15 minutes, moving them about occasionally and watching carefully, especially towards the end of cooking as nuts burn quickly and seemingly without warning. Coconut and oats can be treated in the same way.

Dried Fruit

As with nuts, the fresher the better. As a preference, buy dried fruit at a wholefood shop with a good selection and a regular turnover, as this is likely to be fresher than the packaged fruit (and nuts) found

in the supermarket. (This is also true for nuts and special grains as well.) You are also much more likely to find fruits that have not been treated with sulphur in the wholefood shop. Try to avoid fruit drying out by storing it in the appropriate containers and always sealing the packet when you put it away. To rehydrate fruit, seep it in hot water for about 10 to 15 minutes.

Candied Fruit

This is best bought in specialist cook shops as it is much better than the bulk variety bought in the supermarket at holiday times.

Oats and Muesli

Do not confuse quick oats with rolled oats. Quick oats are rolled oats that have been chopped finely and they therefore absorb more liquid during cooking. Stick to the type that is specified in your particular recipe. Usually, the recipes call for plain muesli without fruit unless otherwise stated.

Flavourings

Spices loose the intensity of their flavour surprisingly quickly, so they need replacing frequently. To prolong their life, keep them in a cool, dark place and certainly out of direct sunlight. Make sure you use only pure vanilla essence – artificial flavouring just does not come close to the real thing. Similarly, freshly squeezed lemon and orange juice (rather than juices out of a carton) and freshly grated citrus zests are an absolute must if you want your cookies to taste truly home-made.

Prepare that Tin

There are several schools of thought with regard to pan preparation. Some prefer to very lightly brush their baking trays with a little oil using a pastry brush or mister spray, and find that is sufficient to stop their cookies from sticking. Others grease with shortening using kitchen towel. However, avoid butter as it burns at a relatively low temperature and salted butter tends to make cookies stick to the tray. You can line the trays with aluminium foil, which needs a little oil, or with nonstick parchment or paper silicone, which do not. Both paper types can be wiped clean after use with kitchen towel and reused several times.

A more recent invention is a very lightweight, flexible silicone mat that can replace parchment lining paper and be reused almost endlessly. These are particularly good for very thin, delicate cookies such as gingerbread men and cut shapes. Liners made of the same material are now also available for baking tins.

Using liners allows you to prepare all the cookies at once, then simply slide onto the baking trays as soon as they become available. Never slide a liner of prepared cookies onto a warm baking tray. The liner must be absolutely cold before it is reused or the fat in the cookies will melt and the cookies spread before they reach the hot air of the oven.

Into the Oven

The oven must be preheated before you put your cookies in to bake. Most ovens take around 10 minutes to heat up to the required temperature, so switch your oven on as soon as you begin your preparation. Every oven is different – consequently, the times given in this book may be a little different from those needed for your own oven. Trust your eyes and your common sense. If you persistently find the timings at variance, test the temperature of your oven accurately using a cooking thermometer; alternatively call for an engineer to check that it is working properly.

For optimum heat circulation, cook on one tray at a time in the centre of the oven. If you cook on two trays at the same time, then reverse the trays halfway through the cooking time to compensate, working quickly to prevent the oven temperature falling too dramatically when you open the oven door. When cooking on two baking trays at once, the cookies will also need a little extra cooking time. For evenly cooked cookies, space as directed in the recipe for consistent air circulation.

15

Day Long Cookies

Cookies can be the perfect snack from dawn to dusk – it's just a matter of choosing the right recipe. From breakfasts on the go to after-dinner treats, there is something for everyone in this selection.

Day Long Cookies

When time is short in the morning, what could be better than a home-baked cookie? Our selection of guilt-free breakfast cookies gives you the energy boost you need to start the day. Make a batch, wrap them in waxed paper and pop them in a bag, then you're ready to grab and run. They make a great solution for ensuring that stay-in-bed kids get a healthy start to the day.

Our selection includes several that take cereals as their base, such as the Granola Bars packed with natural goodness, and fun and funky Peanut and Lemon Crunch Bars. For the European approach try the Chocolate Swirls, or if it is fruit you crave, the Double Banana Cookies or Pear Cookies will hit the spot. Don't save these treats for breakfast time – they are perfect for lunchboxes too.

Later in the day a Honey and Oat Cookie, a delicious Apple and Cinnamon Cookie or an old-fashioned thumbprint could well be the pick-me-up you need to keep you going. And, when the day is done, a little sweet treat after dinner makes the perfect end to a busy day. The No-Bake Chocolate Delights will hit the spot with little effort, while the classy Mini Florentines will impress even the most demanding guests.

Granola Bars

Ideal for those who need to eat breakfast on the move. Grab a bar and a piece of fruit and this will set you up for the day.

Preparation time: 15 minutes
Cooking time: 25 minutes

75g clear/runny honey
115g margarine
55g packed dark brown sugar
55g light brown sugar
225g rolled oats
3 tbsp flaked almonds
3 tbsp chopped walnuts
50g raisins
50g chopped dried dates
80g chopped dried apricots

TIP

Try using 430g of your favourite unsweetened muesli instead of the oats, nuts and dried fruit.

Preheat oven to 180°C (gas mark 4). Grease a shallow 28 x 18cm baking tin or line with a sheet of nonstick baking parchment.

Gently melt the honey, margarine and sugars in a saucepan until well combined, taking care not to boil the mixture. Stir in the oats, nuts and dried fruits, mixing well.

Press the mixture into the baking tin and bake in the centre of the oven for about 25 minutes, until golden. Leave to cool in the tin for 5 minutes. Cut into bars.

Leave to cool completely before removing granola bars from the tin. Store in an airtight container.

Makes 12

Maple Syrup Cookies

These simple cookies are delicately flavoured with maple syrup.

Preparation time: 15 minutes
Cooking time: 12–15 minutes

115g lightly salted butter
115g light brown sugar
1 egg, beaten
170g plain flour
2 tbsp maple syrup

Preheat oven to 180°C (gas mark 4). Grease two large baking trays or line with nonstick baking parchment.

Beat the butter and sugar together in a mixing bowl. Beat in the egg, then add the flour and maple syrup.

Put 12–14 equal-sized spoonfuls of the mixture onto the baking trays, allowing 8cm for spreading. Flatten the mounds of mixture a little with the back of the spoon. Bake in the oven for about 12–15 minutes, until pale golden. Remove from the oven and let cool for a minute to allow the cookies to firm, before removing with a thin metal spatula to a wire rack to cool completely. Store in an airtight container.

Makes 12–14

> ### TIP
> Maple syrup is a natural product and has a finer flavour than the imitation maple-flavoured syrup that is available. But, for reasons of economy, the latter may be used successfully here, too.

Apricot Slices

The fresh tang of apricots combined with comforting oats makes this a great breakfast cookie.

Preparation time: 45 minutes
Cooking time: 25–30 minutes

80g dried apricots
2 tbsp granulated sugar
160ml unsweetened apple juice
115g plain flour
1 tsp bicarbonate of soda
115g rolled oats
55g light brown sugar
115g lightly salted butter

> **TIP**
>
> Dates may be substituted for the apricots but add the bicarbonate of soda when cooking the dates, not with the flour.

Preheat oven to 190°C (gas mark 5). Grease a shallow 28 x 18cm baking tin or line with nonstick baking parchment.

Chop the apricots into quarters and put in a saucepan with the granulated sugar and apple juice. Bring to the boil, cover and simmer for 15 minutes or until the apricots have softened and nearly absorbed all of the apple juice. Leave to cool completely, then put in a blender and process until smooth.

Mix together the flour, bicarbonate of soda, oats and brown sugar in a mixing bowl. Blend in the butter using fingertips, until the mixture resembles bread crumbs.

Press half of the crumbly oat mixture over the base of the baking tin. Spread the apricot purée evenly over the oat mixture, using a thin metal spatula wetted with a little cold water to help ease spreading. Cover with the remaining oat mixture, pressing the mixture down lightly. Bake in the oven for 25–30 minutes, until pale golden. Leave to cool in the pan before cutting into 12 equal-sized bars. Store in an airtight container.

Makes about 12

Pumpkin Seed and Bran Cookies

Packed with goodness, try these deliciously crunchy cookies any time of day.

Preparation time: 10 minutes
Cooking time: 10–12 minutes

115g lightly salted butter
50g ~~115g~~ light brown sugar
100g ~~115g~~ packed dark brown sugar
1 egg, beaten
150g plain flour
60g ~~40g~~ bran
50g pumpkin seeds

Preheat oven to 180°C (gas mark 4). Grease two large baking trays or line with nonstick baking parchment.

Beat the butter and sugars together in a mixing bowl until the mixture turns pale and fluffy. Beat in the egg, then carefully mix in the flour and bran. Stir in three-quarters of the pumpkin seeds.

Put 12 equal-sized spoonfuls of the mixture onto the baking trays, allowing 8cm for spreading. Flatten the mounds of mixture a little with the back of the spoon and sprinkle the remaining pumpkin seeds evenly over the cookies.

Bake for about 10–12 minutes, until golden and just firm. Remove from the oven and let cool for a minute to allow the cookies to firm, then remove with a thin metal spatula to a wire rack to cool completely. Store in an airtight container.

Makes 12

Honey and Oat Cookies

Sweet and delicious honey and oats in a cookie jar breakfast.

Preparation time: 15 minutes
Cooking time: 10–12 minutes

115g lightly salted butter
115g light brown sugar
2 tbsp clear honey
1 egg yolk
170g plain flour
1 tsp baking powder
pinch mixed spice
60g rolled oats

TIP

Do be sure to use rolled oats in this recipe – because they are steamed, rolled and flaked, they cook very quickly.

Preheat the oven to 180˚C (gas mark 4). Meanwhile, grease two large baking trays.

Beat together the butter and sugar in a mixing bowl until pale and fluffy. Beat in the honey and egg yolk, then stir in the flour, baking powder, mixed spice and oats until well combined.

Divide the mixture into 14 equal-sized pieces and roll into balls using your fingertips. Put the cookies onto the baking trays 8cm apart, to allow for spreading. Bake for 10–12 minutes until golden and just firm. Leave to cool for a minute to allow the cookies to firm, before removing with a thin metal spatula to a wire rack to cool. Store in an airtight container.

Makes 14

Cornflake and Sultana Cookies

Soft, chewy cookies that are very easy to make.

Preparation time: 25 minutes
Cooking time: 12–15 minutes

115g soft margarine
115g light brown sugar
1 egg, beaten
150g self-raising flour
40g cornflakes
75g sultanas

TIP

Grape nut cereal could be used instead of cornflakes. Bran flakes will also work, although the result may be less crispy.

Preheat oven to 180°C (gas mark 4). Grease several baking trays or line with nonstick baking parchment.

Beat together the margarine and sugar in a mixing bowl until pale and fluffy. Beat in the egg. Stir in the flour with the cornflakes and sultanas and mix everything together until well combined.

Put mounds of the mixture onto the baking trays, leaving big spaces in between to allow for spreading.

Bake the cookies in the oven for 12–15 minutes, until golden brown. Lift onto wire racks to cool completely. Store in an airtight container.

Makes 18

Double Banana Cookies

These wholesome cookies contain oats, banana chips and fresh chunks of banana.

Preparation time: 25 minutes
Cooking time: 12–15 minutes

115g soft margarine
115g light brown sugar
1 egg, beaten
170g self-raising flour
60g porridge oats
115g chopped candied pineapple
30g crumbled banana chips
1 banana, chopped

Preheat oven to 180°C (gas mark 4). Grease several baking trays or line with nonstick baking parchment.

In a mixing bowl beat together the margarine and sugar until pale and fluffy. Beat in the egg. Stir in the flour with the oats, glacé pineapple, banana chips and fresh banana and mix everything together until well combined.

Put mounds of the mixture onto the baking trays, leaving big spaces in between to allow for spreading.

Bake the cookies in the oven for 12–15 minutes, until golden brown. Lift onto wire racks to cool completely. Store in an airtight container.

Makes 16

Spritz Cookies

A very tangy cookie that never loses its appeal. These make a good-sized batch and are great for brunches or parties.

Preparation time: 40 minutes
Cooking time: 10–15 minutes

350g plain flour	1 egg
½ tsp mixed spice	grated zest of 1 orange
¼ tsp salt	50ml fresh orange juice
170g unsalted butter	½ tsp almond essence
75g caster sugar	pink sugar, to decorate

TIP

These cookies are also called Swedish Butter Cookies or Pressed Butter Cookies. The word Spritz comes from the German word meaning 'to squirt', and this is exactly how they are made.

Preheat oven to 190°C (gas mark 5). In a medium bowl, sift together flour, spice and salt. In a large bowl beat butter until creamy. Add the sugar and continue beating until light and fluffy. Beat in egg, orange zest, freshly squeezed orange juice and almond essence until well blended. Stir in flour until well combined.

Divide the dough into quarters. Working with one quarter at a time, fill a piping bag with a fluted nozzle and pipe small kisses of dough onto a greased baking tray. Bake for 10–15 minutes. Remove from oven and dust with coloured sugar.

Makes about 96

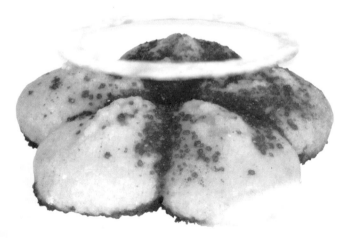

Thumbprints

A cookie classic. Using a selection of jams makes a plate of these look really pretty.

Preparation time: 20 minutes + 1 hour chilling
Cooking time: 15–17 minutes

140g lightly salted butter
75g light brown sugar
1 egg yolk
225g plain flour
14 tsp seedless fruit jam

TIP

Traditionally these are made with strawberry jam. However, try making them with different coloured jams for variety and presentation.

Grease two large baking trays or line with nonstick baking parchment.

Beat together the butter and sugar until light and fluffy. Beat in the egg yolk and stir in the flour. Cover and refrigerate for about an hour, or until firm enough to handle. Preheat oven to 180°C (gas mark 4), then divide the mixture into 14 equal-sized pieces and roll each into balls using your hands. Put at least 2cm apart on the baking trays. Press your thumb into the centre of each cookie ball to make a hollow indentation.

Bake in the oven for about 10–12 minutes until pale brown and just firm. If the centres of the cookies have risen slightly, gently pat back down with the back of a teaspoon. Fill each hollow with a teaspoon of jam and bake for a further 5 minutes. Remove the cookies and lift them onto a wire rack to cool using a thin metal spatula. Store in an airtight container.

Makes 14

Butter, Currant & Coconut Cookies

These cookies are crisp on the day they are made, but if stored in an airtight container they soften and become quite chewy – they are delicious either way.

Preparation time: 15 minutes + 1 hour chilling
Cooking time: 8–10 minutes

230g lightly salted butter
170g light brown sugar
170g self-raising flour
75g dessicated coconut
115g currants

Preheat oven to 200°C (gas mark 6). Grease two large baking trays or line with nonstick baking parchment.

Beat together the butter and sugar in a mixing bowl until pale and fluffy. Beat in the flour and coconut. Stir in the currants. Cover the dough and chill in the refrigerator for about 1 hour to firm.

Form the cookie dough into a roll about 6cm in diameter. Cut into 1cm slices and set well apart to allow for spreading as the cookies double in size. Reshape into neat rounds, if necessary.

Bake the cookies in batches in the oven for about 8–10 minutes, until light brown. Allow to cool for 5 minutes to firm on the baking trays, before removing with a thin metal spatula to a wire rack to cool completely.

Makes 16

Pear Cookies

You will want to add dried pears to many more recipes after enjoying these cookies. Other dried fruits, such as apricots, can also be substituted.

Preparation time: 15 minutes
Cooking time: 12–14 minutes

115g lightly salted butter
115g light brown sugar
1 egg, beaten
170g plain flour
140g chopped dried pears

Preheat oven to 180°C (gas mark 4). Grease two large baking trays or line with nonstick baking parchment.

Beat the butter and sugar together in a mixing bowl until pale and fluffy. Beat in the egg and flour. Stir in the chopped pears.

Put 12–14 equal-sized spoonfuls of the cookie mixture onto the baking trays, allowing 5–8cm for spreading. Flatten the mounds of mixture a little using the back of the spoon. Bake the cookies in the oven for about 12–14 minutes, until pale golden. Remove from the oven and leave to firm on the baking trays for a minute, before removing with a thin metal spatula to a wire rack to cool completely. Store in an airtight container.

Makes 12–14

Chocolate Swirls

Using ready-made puff pastry makes this a very quick and easy recipe.

Preparation time: 5 minutes
Cooking time: 10–12 minutes

225g ready-made and rolled puff pastry, thawed if frozen
3–4 tbsp chocolate spread

Preheat oven to 220°C (gas mark 7). Grease two large baking trays or line with nonstick baking parchment.

Put the puff pastry on a lightly floured surface and, if necessary, roll to make a rectangle measuring 28 x 23cm. Spread the chocolate spread evenly all over the surface of the pastry. Holding one of the short sides, roll the pastry up to make a long roll. Cut across the pastry roll with a sharp knife to make 5mm-thick slices.

Transfer the pastry swirls onto the baking trays, allowing a little space for spreading. If necessary, reshape into neat circles and pat down slightly. Bake for 8 minutes in the centre of the oven until golden brown, then carefully turn the pastries over and bake for a further 2–4 minutes, until golden. Using a thin metal spatula, remove the chocolate swirls to a wire rack to cool completely.

Makes about 20

TIP

Sprinkle the finely grated zest of a large orange over the chocolate spread before rolling the pastry for a tangy flavour.

Apple and Cinnamon Cookies

These cookies are best eaten the day they are made, but can also be stored in an airtight container for up to two days.

TIP

Work quickly with the apple, preparing it at the last minute, or toss with 1 teaspoon of lemon juice to prevent discolouration.

Preparation time: 15 minutes + 30 minutes chilling
Cooking time: 25 minutes

230g lightly salted butter
115g icing sugar
4 drops vanilla essence
1 tsp ground cinnamon
225g plain flour
155g cornflour
3 tbsp apple sauce
1 eating apple, peeled, cored and chopped

Preheat oven to 180°C (gas mark 4). Grease two large baking trays or line with nonstick baking parchment.

Beat the butter, icing sugar, vanilla and cinnamon until well combined. Stir in the flour, cornflour, apple sauce and diced apple until it forms a well-mixed but crumbly dough. If the mixture is soft and sticky, refrigerate for at least 30 minutes to firm.

Divide the mixture into 12 equal-sized pieces and, using your hands, shape into balls. Put the cookie balls onto the baking trays, 8cm apart, and flatten slightly with a fork. Bake for about 25 minutes, until golden. Leave to cool on the baking trays for 5 minutes to firm before removing with a thin metal spatula to a wire rack to cool completely.

Makes 12

Peanut and Lemon Crunch Bars

Peanut butter is everybody's favourite, and it makes these cookies a nutritious treat.

TIP

These cookies are great in a lunchbox. Don't let the inclusion of breakfast cereals trick you into thinking that they are reserved for mornings only.

Preparation time: 10 minutes + 30 minutes chilling

60g lightly salted butter
55g light brown sugar
3 tbsp honey
3 tbsp crunchy peanut butter
zest of 1 lemon
180g crisp rice breakfast cereal
180g cornflakes

Grease an 20cm-square, shallow baking tin or line with nonstick baking parchment.

Put the butter, sugar, honey and peanut butter into a large saucepan and heat gently to melt the butter and dissolve the sugar. Do not boil the mixture. When the ingredients are melted and well combined, remove from the heat.

Stir the lemon zest, rice cereal and cornflakes into the melted mixture carefully so as not to crush the cereals. Mix well. Spoon the mixture into the tin and level the surface. Leave to set for at least 30 minutes in a cool place, then cut into 6–8 equal-sized bars. Store in an airtight container.

Makes 6–8

Oaties

Delicious with a glass of cold milk in the afternoon, or with your morning coffee, these are a staple for any family kitchen.

Preparation time: 15 minutes
Cooking time: 10 minutes

60g unsalted butter
60g vegetable shortening
115g light brown sugar
50g granulated sugar
1 tsp vanilla essence
1¼ tsps ground cinnamon
⅛ tsp ground nutmeg

½ tsp salt
1 tsp cider or white vinegar
1 large egg
½ tsp bicarbonate of soda
90g plain flour
130g quick-cook rolled oats

TIP

These are endlessly adaptable: dip half of each cookie in melted chocolate, replace ¼ of the oats with dessicated coconut or add in 55g sultanas just before baking.

Preheat oven to 180°C (gas mark 4). Grease two large baking trays or line with nonstick baking parchment.

In a large bowl, beat together the butter, shortening, sugars, vanilla, cinnamon, nutmeg, salt and vinegar until fairly smooth; a few tiny bits of butter may still show. Beat in the egg, and then add the bicarbonate of soda and flour. Add the oats, and stir to combine.

Roll tablespoons of the dough into balls, and place onto the prepared baking trays, about 8cm apart. Flatten each dough ball. For softer cookies, bake for 12–13 minutes; for crunchier cookies, bake for 14–15 minutes, or until golden brown all over. Remove the cookies from the oven, and let cool. Store in an airtight container for up to a week.

Makes about 36

33

No-bake Chocolate Delights

A cross between a cookie and a truffle – and so easy to make.

Preparation time: 15 minutes + 1 hour setting

100g Madeira cake crumbs
85g glacé cherries, quartered
50g raisins
55g plain chocolate
30g lightly salted butter
2 tbsp milk

TIP

Serve these with after-dinner coffee for the perfect end to a meal. Replace the milk with rum to make them extra special.

Put the cake crumbs, quartered cherries and raisins into a mixing bowl. Break the chocolate into small pieces and put in a small heatproof bowl with the butter and milk over a saucepan of hot, but not boiling, water. Carefully melt all of the ingredients and stir into the sponge and fruit mixture. Mix together thoroughly to combine all of the ingredients and then leave to cool for a short while until the mixture is cool enough to handle.

Using a teaspoon, put heaped spoonfuls of mixture on waxed paper in a single layer on a baking tray. Chill the chocolate cookies in the refrigerator for at least 1 hour, to firm. Remove from the waxed paper and store in an airtight container.

Makes about 20

Minute Meringues

Tiny bubbles of airy sugar – irresistible!

Preparation time: 10 minutes
Cooking time: 45 minutes

1 egg white
50g white sugar
⅛ tsp cream of tartar
⅛ tsp salt

Preheat oven to 140˚C (gas mark 1). Line two baking trays with edible rice paper or nonstick baking parchment.

Put the egg white in a grease-free mixing bowl and whisk until soft peaks form. Whisk in half of the sugar and all of the cornflour, until well combined. Add the remaining sugar and whisk until shiny and fairly stiff.

Spoon the meringue mixture carefully into a piping bag fitted with a small nozzle and then pipe small mounds directly onto the lined baking trays, leaving 2cm between them to allow for a little spreading during the cooking process. Bake in the oven for about 45 minutes, until pale brown and crisp. Remove from the oven and cool completely, before removing from the baking parchment. If using rice paper, remove as much as possible, but any left on the base of the meringues will be edible. Store in an airtight container.

Makes about 24

Melting Moments

These literally melt in your mouth, and keep really well. Try adding 2 teaspoons of cinnamon or ground cardamom to the dough before chilling.

Preparation time: 10 minutes
Cooking time: 15 minutes

170g plain flour
55g cornflour
¼ tsp salt
25g icing sugar
230g unsalted butter, room temperature
1 tsp pure vanilla essence
55g caster sugar

In a large bowl, beat together the butter and sugar until light and fluffy. Beat in the vanilla essence. Add the flour mixture mix well. Cover and refrigerate the dough for an hour or two, or until firm.

Preheat oven to 180°C (gas mark 4). Grease two large baking trays or line with nonstick baking parchment.

When batter is firm, form into 2–3cm balls and then shape each ball into a cylinder shape before bending to form horseshoe shapes. Place the caster sugar on a plate, and roll each cookie in the sugar before transferring to the prepared baking trays. Bake for about 10–14 minutes, or until the edges of the cookies just start to brown. Remove from oven and place on a wire rack to cool for a few minutes. Transfer the cookies to a wire rack to cool completely. Store in an airtight container for up to 2 weeks.

Makes about 24

TIP

These can be rolled in oats, flavoured sugar, icing sugar, dessicated coconut or even crushed nuts. Experiment to find your favourite!

Chocolate Pretzels

These delicious pretzels are surprisingly easy to form.

Preparation time: 40 minutes + 2 hours chilling
Cooking time: 10–12 minutes

170g plain flour
¼ tsp salt
3 tbsp unsweetened cocoa powder
115g unsalted butter
55g caster sugar
1 egg, beaten
1 tsp vanilla essence

Glaze
1 egg white, lightly beaten
sugar crystals, for sprinkling

TIP

If you are short of time, or simply impatient, chill the dough in the freezer for 30–45 minutes. Then, keep the bulk of the dough in the refrigerator while shaping the pretzels to prevent it from warming up again.

Sift together the flour, salt and cocoa powder. In a separate bowl, beat the butter until creamy, add the sugar and continue beating until light and fluffy. Beat in the egg and vanilla until well blended. Gradually add the flour mixture until combined. Turn dough onto a piece of cling film and seal. Refrigerate until firm, 1–2 hours.

Preheat oven to 190°C (gas mark 5). Grease two large baking trays or line with nonstick baking parchment.

With lightly floured hands, roll dough into about thirty 4cm balls. Roll each into a 'rope' about 23cm long. Bring each end of the rope together to meet in the centre. Twist the ends together, and press to the middle of the rope to form the pretzel shape. Transfer to the baking trays.

Brush each pretzel with egg white to glaze, then sprinkle with sugar crystals. Bake until firm, 10–12 minutes. Cool and tranfer to wire racks to cool completely. Store in an airtight container.

Makes about 30

Global Cookies

The whole world loves a cookie. We may call them by different names, but there is something universal about the sublime joy of biting into the crunchy, sweet nugget of bliss that we call a cookie.

Global Cookies

The cookie is not a new phenomenon and most countries and many towns have their own treasures much loved by their people. Looking at the selection in this chapter it is clear to see national influences. However, at their heart, most cookies are wonderful confections of butter, sugar, spices, fruits and nuts. They can usually be made ahead of time – take advantage of this and serve them as dessert: Espresso Biscotti after breakfast, Spanish Churros after paella, or offer a Coconut Fortune Cookie after a Chinese stirfry.

We begin with a selection of traditional American cookies. Childhood is filled with Rocky Road, while Peanut Butter and Jelly Cookies are the staple of birthday parties in everyone's memory.

The cookie trail then moves on to Britain, where cookies are more commonly called biscuits and are often laced with ginger or are rich in butter, as typified by Scottish Shortbread. Italians love almonds and their Biscotti are the perfect accompaniment to coffee. Further east there are Polish Macaroons sprinkled with poppy seeds, then head south and you will find Chrabeli, evocative of the eastern Mediterranean. In the Far East there are Jalebi from India and Fortune Cookies from China. Not forgetting the southern hemisphere, we have also included Grated Peach Shortcake and bold Chunky Macadamia Cookies from Australia.

Shoofly Slices

This cookie evolved from the shoofly pies of Pennsylvannia, which in turn had their roots in the British treacle tart.

Preparation time: 40 minutes
Cooking time: 35 minutes

170g plain flour
pinch of salt
2 tbsp icing sugar
115g lightly salted butter

Filling
50ml golden syrup
50ml treacle
150ml boiling water
1 tsp bicarbonate of soda
280g plain flour
1 tsp ground ginger
1 tsp ground cinnamon
115g lightly salted butter
170g light brown sugar

TIP

The curious name of these cookies probably has its origins in the days of the early American settlers, who baked in communal outdoor ovens. Doubtless the sweet smell of molasses (treacle) attracted a great number of flies.

Preheat oven to 180°C (gas mark 4). Lightly grease a 28 x 18cm tin. Sift the flour, salt and icing sugar into a mixing bowl. Blend in the butter until the mixture resembles fine bread crumbs. Add enough cold water to make a firm dough. Roll out on a lightly floured surface and use to line the base and sides of the tin. Chill in the refrigerator while making the filling.

Put the golden syrup and treacle in a heatproof jug and pour over the boiling water. Stir until well mixed, then add the bicarbonate of soda and mix again. Leave to stand for 5 minutes.

Sift the flour, ginger and cinnamon into a bowl. Blend in the butter until the mixture resembles bread crumbs. Stir in the light brown sugar. Spoon half the crumb mixture evenly over the base of the tin. Slowly pour over the syrup and treacle mixture, then spoon over the remaining crumb mixture.

Bake immediately for 35 minutes, or until lightly set. The mixture will rise a little as it cooks, but will sink again as it cools. Leave to cool in the tin. Divide into 14 slices.

Makes 14

Peanut Butter and Jelly Cookies

The popular US combination of peanut butter and jelly (jam) as a sandwich filling appears in these giant crunchy cookies.

Preparation time: 25 minutes + 1 hour chilling
Cooking time: 15 minutes

85g unsalted peanuts
115g unsalted butter
90g caster sugar
75g light brown sugar
1 tbsp seedless raspberry jam
115g smooth or crunchy peanut butter
1 tsp vanilla essence
1 egg, beaten
170g plain flour
2 tsp baking powder

> ## TIP
>
> **Cashew Cookies** Add 115g cashew butter and 85g chopped roasted cashews instead of the peanut butter and the unsalted peanuts.

Lightly grease two baking trays or line with nonstick baking paper. Spread the peanuts on another baking tray and roast in the oven for 5 minutes, until beginning to turn brown. Let cool, then roughly chop.

Beat the butter and sugars until light and fluffy. Add the jam, peanut butter and vanilla, then beat until thoroughly mixed. Gradually add the egg, a little at a time, beating well after each addition. Sift the flour and baking powder into the bowl. Stir into the mixture with the chopped nuts to make a soft dough. Wrap the dough in cling film and chill in the refrigerator for 1 hour.

Preheat oven to 180°C (gas mark 4). Divide the dough into 24 pieces. Roll each piece into a ball the size of a walnut. Put the cookies onto the prepared baking trays, spacing well apart. Flatten slightly with a fork. Bake for 15 minutes or until golden brown. Leave on the baking trays for 3–4 minutes, then remove with a thin metal spatula and cool on a wire rack.

Makes 24

Rocky Road

Both children and adults love this sumptuously wicked treat.

Preparation time: 25 minutes
Cooking time: 10 minutes

90g plain flour
2 tbsp unsweetened cocoa powder
scant 25g icing sugar
60g lightly salted butter
1 egg yolk
1 tbsp milk

Topping
400g plain chocolate
60g unsalted butter
60g glacé cherries
150g mini marshmallows
40g unsalted peanuts

> **TIP**
>
> Use white chocolate for an extra-special Rocky Road. You could also substitute 50g each of plain and milk chocolate chips for the 150g marshmallows.

Preheat oven to 180°C (gas mark 4). Grease and line the base of a 28 x 18cm tin with nonstick baking parchment.

Sift the flour, cocoa powder and sugar into a bowl. Cut the butter into small pieces and blend in until the mixture resembles bread crumbs. Add the egg yolk and milk to the dry ingredients and mix to a firm dough. Knead on a lightly floured surface until smooth, then press into the base of the tin. Prick all over with a fork, then bake for 10 minutes. Let cool while making the topping.

Break the chocolate into pieces and put in a bowl with the butter over a saucepan of near-boiling water. Heat gently until melted, stirring occasionally. Remove from the heat and let cool for 3 minutes. While the chocolate is melting, snip the cherries into quarters with oiled scissors. Stir into the chocolate along with the mini marshmallows and peanuts.

Quickly pour the topping over the base, gently shaking the tin to spread the mixture. Leave to set at room temperature. Cut into 18 small squares and store in the refrigerator until ready to serve.

Makes 18

Refrigerator Cookies

Also known as freezer cookies, this cookie dough will keep for up to a week in the refrigerator. It freezes well too so you can make it ahead of time and bake as necessary.

TIP

These simple cookies have scope for plenty of variations. Try using the grated zest of a lemon and a teaspoon of lemon juice instead of vanilla, or simply add a few finely chopped nuts or dried apricots to the dough.

Preparation time: 20 minutes + 1–2 hours chilling
Cooking time: 10–12 minutes

225g plain flour
1 tsp baking powder
115g lightly salted butter

55g caster sugar
1 egg
½ tsp vanilla essence

Sift the flour and baking powder into a mixing bowl. Cut the butter into small pieces and blend in until the mixture resembles bread crumbs. Stir in the sugar. Beat the egg with the vanilla, add to the dry ingredients and mix to a firm dough. Shape into a roll about 5cm in diameter and wrap in cling film or foil. Chill in the refrigerator for 1–2 hours until very firm, or until needed.

When ready to bake the cookies, preheat oven to 190°C (gas mark 5). Lightly grease three baking trays or line with nonstick baking parchment.

Unwrap the dough and cut into 5mm slices. Arrange on the baking trays, spacing well apart. Bake for 10–12 minutes or until golden brown. Leave on the baking trays for 5 minutes, then transfer to a wire rack to cool.

Makes 40

Grantham Gingerbreads

These crisp, pale spiced cookies are also known as 'white buttons' in the Norfolk fenlands, where they are often rolled in sugar after cooking.

Preparation time: 15 minutes
Cooking time: 35 minutes

115g lightly salted butter
350g caster sugar
1 egg, beaten

250g self-raising flour
1 tsp ground ginger
¼ tsp ground cinnamon

TIP

For a spicier version of these cookies, sprinkle with 2 tablespoons caster sugar mixed with ¼ teaspoon each of ground ginger and ground cinnamon before baking.

Preheat oven to 150°C (gas mark 2). Lightly grease two baking trays or line with nonstick baking parchment.

Beat the butter and sugar together until pale and fluffy. Gradually add the egg, beating well after each addition. Sift the flour and spices into the mixture and work in to make a firm dough.

Roll into small walnut-sized balls and put on the prepared baking trays, spacing slightly apart. Press down slightly on each ball. Bake for 35 minutes, or until well risen, crisp and light golden. Leave on the cookie sheets for 2–3 minutes, then remove and cool on a wire rack.

Makes 25

Wholemeal Rounds

These very traditional savoury cookies are sometimes spread with butter and served with cheese. The amount of sugar may be varied, depending how sweet you like them.

TIP

Pricking the dough with a fork prevents it from bubbling as the cookies bake.

Preparation time: 20 minutes
Cooking time: 20 minutes

225g plain wholemeal flour
55g fine oatmeal
½ tsp salt
60g lightly salted butter
60g shortening

4 tbsp light brown sugar
½ beaten egg
2 tbsp milk
2 tbsp fine oatmeal, for sprinkling

Preheat oven to 180°C (gas mark 4). Lightly grease two baking trays or line with nonstick baking parchment.

Put the flour, oatmeal and salt in a bowl and stir together. Blend in the butter and shortening until the mixture resembles fine bread crumbs. Stir in the sugar. Add the beaten egg and mix to a firm dough. Lightly knead for a few seconds until smooth.

Roll out the dough to 3mm thickness on a floured surface. Cut into rounds using a 6cm plain cutter and lift onto the prepared baking trays.

Brush the rounds very lightly with milk and sprinkle with the oatmeal. Prick all over with a fork and bake for 20 minutes, until slightly darkened. Leave on the baking trays for 2 minutes, then remove and cool on a wire rack.

Makes 20

Scottish Shortbread

Generations of Scots have baked this simple delicious cookie. As with all 'traditional' recipes there are many variations, but these are always made with butter.

Preparation time: 15 minutes + 1 hour chilling
Cooking time: 35–40 minutes

115g lightly salted butter
2 tbsp caster sugar
150g plain flour
3 tbsp ground rice
1 tbsp caster sugar, for dusting

Lightly grease a baking tray or line with nonstick baking parchment.

Put the butter in a mixing bowl and beat until soft and creamy. Stir in the sugar. Sift in the flour and mix in with the semolina, or ground rice. Lightly knead on a floured surface for a few seconds until smooth.

Roll out the dough to a 15cm circle, then press into a 18cm shortbread mould. Unmould onto the prepared baking tray. Alternatively, press into a 18cm springform cake tin. Prick all over and mark out 8 wedges. Chill in the refrigerator for 1 hour.

Preheat oven to 170°C (gas mark 3). Bake for 35–40 minutes, or until pale golden brown. Remove from the oven and dust with caster sugar. Leave on the baking tray or remove from the tin, leaving the shortbread on the base for 15 minutes, then cool on a wire rack. Store in an airtight container.

Makes 8 wedges

TIP

Bake your shortbread in the top third of the oven. This will ensure that the top and bottom are evenly cooked.

Amaretti

Wrap these after-dinner almond cookies in pairs with pretty pastel tissue paper for an authentic presentation.

Preparation time: 15 minutes
Cooking time: 12 minutes

1 egg white
2 tsp amaretto liqueur
¼ tsp almond essence
170g ground almonds
115g icing sugar
2 tbsp icing sugar, for dusting

TIP

Amaretto is a sweet almond liqueur. An orange or coffee liqueur may also be used in its place.

Preheat oven to 180°C (gas mark 4). Line two baking trays with nonstick baking parchment.

Lightly whisk the egg white with a fork until slightly frothy. Add the amaretto liqueur and almond essence and whisk again.

Put the almond meal in a bowl and sift in the icing sugar. Make a well in the middle, add the egg white mixture, and stir to a stiff dough. Divide the dough into 30 pieces, then roll each into a ball. Put on the prepared baking trays, spacing slightly apart.

Bake for 12 minutes, or until the cookies are golden brown. Dust with icing sugar. Leave on the baking trays for 2 minutes, then transfer to a wire rack to cool.

Makes 30

Espresso Biscotti

The name of these crisp Italian cookies means 'twice baked'. They're wonderful served with steaming black coffee or cappuccino, although traditionally they are dipped into chilled sweet wine.

Preparation time: 20 minutes
Cooking time: 30 minutes

75g unblanched almonds
250g plain flour
1½ tsp baking powder
pinch of salt
85g unsalted butter

90g caster sugar
2 eggs, beaten
2 tbsp strong espresso coffee, cooled

TIP

Look out for Vin Santo – this is the sweet dessert wine from Tuscany that is frequently used to accompany biscotti.

Preheat oven to 180°C (gas mark 4) Lightly grease a baking tray or line with nonstick baking parchment.

Put the almonds on another baking tray and roast in the oven for 5 minutes. Let cool, then grind in a food processor until fine.

Sift the flour, baking powder and salt into a mixing bowl. Cut the butter into small pieces and blend into the flour until the mixture resembles bread crumbs. Stir in the sugar and ground almonds. Make a well in the middle. Mix the egg and coffee together and add to the dry ingredients. Mix to a firm dough.

Lightly knead on a floured surface for a few seconds until smooth, then shape into two rolls about 6cm in diameter. Transfer to the prepared baking tray and bake for 20 minutes until lightly browned. Leave to cool for 5 minutes, then cut with a serrated knife into 1cm slices. Arrange on the baking tray, cut side down, and bake for a further 10 minutes, until golden brown and dry to the touch. Store the biscotti in an airtight container for at least 24 hours, before serving.

Makes 20

Spanish Churros

These are freshly made and sold as a snack on street stalls throughout Spain to be eaten while you stroll along.

Preparation time: 15 minutes
Cooking time: 10 minutes

85g slightly salted butter
1 cup water
1 cup plain flour
3 tbsp caster sugar
3 eggs
oil for deep frying

> ### TIP
> If you prefer, you may dust the churros with icing sugar mixed together with a little ground cinnamon instead of the caster sugar.

Put the butter and water in a saucepan and heat gently until melted. Meanwhile, sift the flour and ½ teaspoon of the sugar onto a piece of greaseproof paper.

Bring the butter and water to a fast boil, then add the sifted flour and sugar all at once. Remove the pan from the heat and beat vigorously. Leave to cool for 5 minutes.

Lightly beat the eggs and gradually add to the mixture, beating until very smooth and glossy. Spoon the mixture into a piping bag fitted with a 1cm star nozzle.

Half fill a pan with oil and heat to 190°C (gas mark 5). Pipe five 10cm lengths of the mixture at a time into the hot oil. Fry for about 2 minutes, or until golden and crisp. Remove from the oil with slotted spoon and drain on kitchen towel. Repeat until all the mixture is used up. Serve warm or cold, dredged with remaining sugar.

Makes about 25

Piroulines

These crisp, cigar-shaped cookies, originally from Belgium, make a delicious accompaniment to ice creams and mousses.

Preparation time: 20 minutes
Cooking time: 5–6 minutes per batch

60g unsalted butter
2 egg whites
90g caster sugar
55g plain flour
½ tsp vanilla essence

> **TIP**
> Try dipping the tips of the cooled cookies into melted dark chocolate and then leaving them to set on greaseproof paper.

Preheat oven to 190°C (gas mark 5). Line a baking tray with nonstick baking parchment.

Melt the butter over a low heat, then leave to cool. Whisk the egg whites until stiff peaks form. Gradually add the sugar a tablespoon at a time, whisking between each addition. Sift half the flour over the whisked mixture and trickle the melted butter around the edge. Carefully fold in. Sift the remaining flour over the mixture and fold in with the vanilla essence.

Drop teaspoonfuls of the mixture onto the prepared baking tray, spacing well apart. Spread the mixture thinly and evenly to form circles 10cm in diameter. Bake for 5–6 minutes, or until golden brown around the edges. It is best to bake only three or four piroulines at a time as they need to be rolled quickly while warm, before the mixture hardens.

Using a metal spatula, carefully remove the cookies one at a time from the baking tray while still hot. Roll immediately around the oiled handle of a wooden spoon. Remove and leave on a wire rack to cool. Repeat with the remaining cookie mixture until used up.

Makes about 25

Sablés Nantais

These cookies come from the French region of Nantes. 'Sable' is French for 'sand', and reflects their golden crumbly texture.

Preparation time: 25 minutes + 1 hour chilling
Cooking time: 15 minutes

115g unsalted butter	1 tsp vanilla essence
115g icing sugar	170g plain flour
1 egg, separated	¼ tsp baking powder
1 egg yolk	

Put the butter in a mixing bowl and beat until soft. Sift over the icing sugar and beat the mixture until light and fluffy. Beat in the egg yolks, one at a time, then beat in the vanilla. Sift the flour and baking powder over the butter mixture and mix to a soft dough. Lightly knead on a floured surface for a few seconds until smooth. Cover with cling film and chill in the refrigerator for 1 hour.

Preheat oven to 190°C (gas mark 5). Lightly grease two baking trays or line with nonstick baking parchment.

Roll out the cookie dough on a floured surface to a 5mm thickness and stamp out rounds using a fluted 5cm cutter. Transfer to the prepared baking trays.

Lightly beat the egg white. Mark criss-cross patterns on top of the cookies with the back of a knife or with a fork. Brush with the egg white, then bake for 15 minutes, until golden brown. Leave on the baking trays for 3 minutes, then transfer to a wire rack to cool.

Makes 25

TIP

If your dough crumbles as you roll it, it is probably too dry. To remedy, simply add a little softened butter or milk, knead lightly, wrap then re-chill before using.

Eponges

'Eponges' is the French word for sponge and is thought to be the name given to these cookies because they look like sea sponges.

Preparation time: 25 minutes
Cooking time: 9–10 minutes

2 egg whites
2 tbsp caster sugar
55g icing sugar
55g ground almonds
scant 115g blanched almonds, finely chopped
¼ cup seedless raspberry jam
1 tbsp icing sugar, to dust

Preheat oven to 190°C (gas mark 5). Line two baking trays with nonstick baking parchment.

Whisk the egg whites until soft peaks form, then gradually add the caster sugar, whisking after each addition until the mixture is stiff and glossy.

Sift the icing sugar and ground almonds together and fold in. Spoon the mixture into a piping bag fitted with a 1cm plain nozzle and pipe small rounds onto the baking trays, spacing them slightly apart.

Sprinkle with the chopped almonds and bake for 9–10 minutes, until golden. The eponges will rise slightly during cooking, and shrink again as they cool. Remove from the baking trays and cool on a wire rack. When cool, sandwich together in pairs with the jam. Dust with icing sugar before serving. Eponges are best eaten on the day they are made.

Makes 20

TIP

You could also try sandwiching these together with chocolate-hazelnut spread.

Chrabeli

These crisp and light Mediterranean cookies are usually served with black coffee or eaten as a simple snack. Before baking they're left on the baking tray to dry overnight, then stored in the biscuit tin for at least a week.

Preparation time: 20 minutes + 1 hour standing
Cooking time: 10 minutes

3 egg whites
55g icing sugar
150g plain flour
4 tbsp cornflour

TIP

There is a classic anise version of these. Add 1½ teaspoons of aniseed, a pinch of salt, 1 tablespoon kirsch (cherry brandy) and an extra 2 tablespoons of flour to the dough.

Put the egg whites in a large mixing bowl. Sift the icing sugar over the egg whites, then whisk until the mixture will hold stiff peaks.

Sift over the flour and gently fold in until combined, taking care not to over-mix. Cover the bowl with a damp cloth and leave for 1 hour.

Line two baking trays with nonstick baking parchment, then lightly dust with the cornflour. Knead the dough on a lightly floured surface for a minute or so until smooth.

Take walnut-sized pieces of the mixture and shape into ovals. Using scissors, snip three cuts down one side, then put on the prepared sheets, bending the cookies slightly to open up the cuts. Keep dipping your hands in flour when shaping the cookies, to prevent them from sticking. Leave uncovered overnight to let the cookies dry out.

The following day, preheat oven to 200°C (gas mark 6). Bake the cookies for 10 minutes, until very pale brown. Remove from the baking trays and cool on a wire rack at least overnight, and for up to three days.

Makes 25

Polish Macaroons

These 'Makaroniki' could be sprinkled with poppy seeds instead of the flaked almonds for a delicious alternative.

Preparation time: 25 minutes
Cooking time: 15–20 minutes

85g blanched almonds
200g caster sugar
2 tbsp cornflour
2 egg whites
¼ tsp almond essence, optional
¼ cup flaked almonds
rice paper

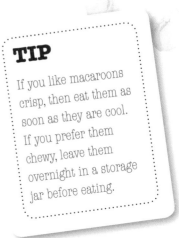

TIP

If you like macaroons crisp, then eat them as soon as they are cool. If you prefer them chewy, leave them overnight in a storage jar before eating.

Preheat oven to 190°C (gas mark 5). Line two baking trays with rice paper.

Spread the blanched almonds on a tray and roast for 5 minutes, or until just beginning to brown. Allow to cool, then grind finely in a nut grinder or food processor.

Mix together the ground almonds, sugar and cornflour. Lightly whisk the egg whites and add to the dry ingredients, with the almond essence if using, to make a thick paste.

Spoon the mixture into a piping bag fitted with a plain 1cm nozzle. Pipe 16 rounds of the mixture on the prepared baking trays, spacing well apart. Sprinkle each with a few flaked almonds. Bake for 15–20 minutes, or until lightly browned. Leave on the baking trays for 5 minutes, then remove and cool on a wire rack. Tear away any excess rice paper when cold.

Makes 16

Grated Peach Shortcake

It's not the peaches that are grated in this chunky Australian slice, but the buttery shortcake that sandwiches it together.

Preparation time: 20 minutes + 15 minutes chilling
Cooking time: 45 minutes

230g lightly salted butter
75g light brown sugar
1 egg
1 tbsp sunflower oil
1 tsp vanilla essence
400g plain flour

25g cornflour
2 tsp baking powder
115g dried peaches
3 tbsp peach or orange juice
140g peach or apricot jam

TIP

Grated Pineapple Shortcake Substitute glacé pineapple pieces for the dried peaches, simmered in pineapple juice, and use pineapple jam instead of peach or apricot.

Lightly grease and line the base of a round 20cm springform tin.

Beat the butter until creamy, then add the light brown sugar and mix until light and fluffy. Beat the egg, oil and vanilla together. Gradually add to the butter mixture, beating well between each addition. Sift the flour, cornflour and baking powder together. Stir into the butter mixture to make a stiff dough. Knead on a lightly floured surface until smooth. Wrap and chill the dough in the refrigerator for 15 minutes.

Meanwhile, finely chop the peaches and put in a small saucepan with the fruit juice. Heat gently for 3–4 minutes, until the fruit juice is absorbed. Remove from the heat and stir in the jam.

Preheat oven to 150°C (gas mark 2). Cut the dough in two and coarsely grate one half into the prepared tin, covering the base evenly. Spoon over the warm peach mixture. Grate the rest of the cookie dough evenly over the top.

Bake for 45 minutes or until lightly browned. Leave to cool in the tin. Cut the shortcake into wedges to serve.

Makes 8 wedges

Chunky Macadamia Cookies

Macadamia trees are native to the woodlands of Australia and produce small, white, buttery nuts.

TIP

Chocolate Macadamia Cookies Substitute 25g unsweetened cocoa powder for 25g of the flour.

Preparation time: 20 minutes
Cooking time: 12–15 minutes

60g unsalted butter
60g shortening
115g light brown sugar
1 egg, beaten

225g plain flour
½ tsp baking powder
85g macadamia nuts
4 tbsp milk

Preheat oven to 180°C (gas mark 4). Lightly grease two baking trays or line with nonstick baking parchment.

Put the butter and shortening in a mixing bowl and beat until soft. Add the light brown sugar and cream together until light and fluffy. Gradually add the egg, beating well between each addition.

Sift the flour and baking powder into the bowl and fold into the butter mixture with the nuts and milk to make a fairly firm dough. Put small teaspoonfuls of the mixture onto the prepared baking trays, spacing well apart. Bake for 12–15 minutes, until light golden brown. Leave for 5 minutes, then transfer to a wire rack to cool completely.

Makes about 25

Jalebi

These Indian batter coils are deep-fried, then soaked in a saffron and cardamom syrup.

Preparation time: 20 minutes +
  2 hours standing
Cooking time: 20 minutes

225g plain flour
7g easy-blend dried yeast
55g plain yoghurt
300ml warm water
sunflower oil for deep-frying

Syrup
200g granulated sugar
large pinch saffron strands
6 cardamom pods, lightly crushed
300ml water

TIP

In India, they pour their batter into the hot oil using a coconut with a hole in it. If using a spoon is too difficult, you might find it easier to form the thin, coiled circles using a ketchup dispenser.

Sift the flour into a bowl and stir in the easy-blend dried yeast. Make a well in the middle. Add the yoghurt and water and gradually blend in the flour to make a thick batter. Cover the bowl with a tea towel and leave the batter for 2 hours.

Meanwhile, make the syrup. Put the sugar, saffron and cardamom pods in a pan with the water. Heat gently, stirring occasionally until the sugar dissolves. Bring to the boil and simmer for 1 minute. Strain the syrup into a bowl.

Half-fill a deep saucepan with oil and heat to 190°C (gas mark 5). Stir the batter, then pour through a basting spoon in a steady stream into the oil to form coils, making four or five at a time. Deep fry for about 30 seconds, then turn over and continue cooking until deep golden. Remove from the pan and drain on kitchen towel, then immerse in the sugar syrup for 2–3 minutes. Repeat with remaining batter and syrup until used up. Serve straight away.

Makes 16–20

Coconut Fortune Cookies

Everyone knows these Chinese cookies. This version has a delicate texture, provided by a little grated coconut.

Preparation time: 30 minutes
Cooking time: 5 minutes

2 egg whites
55g icing sugar, sifted
1 tsp coconut or almond essence
2 tbsp unsalted butter, melted
5 tbsp plain flour, sifted
15g finely grated coconut, toasted and chopped

TIP

If you want to add fortunes, write on small pieces of paper, then slip into the hot cookies before folding them in half.

Grease and flour two baking trays. Using a glass or cutter, mark 8cm circles on the baking tray, spaced well apart to allow cookies to spread.

In a medium bowl, beat the egg whites until foamy. Gradually beat in icing sugar, coconut or almond essence, and melted butter. Fold in the flour until well blended.

Drop a teaspoonful of batter in the centre of each marked circle and, using the back of a spoon, spread evenly to cover the circle. Sprinkle each cookie with a little toasted coconut.

Bake one sheet at a time until the edges are lightly browned, about 5 minutes. Remove the baking tray to a wire rack and, working quickly, use a thin-bladed metal spatula to loosen the edges of each cookie. Set on a board and fold in half, then curve each cookie over the rim of a glass creating the classic shape. Hold for 30 seconds, then put on a wire rack to cool completely. Repeat with the remaining cookies. If the cookies become too firm, return to the oven for 30 seconds.

Makes about 12

Cookies for Giving

What better to give than lovingly made cookies? These ambrosial gifts are the way to show you really care, with a personal touch no shop-bought gift can match.

Cookies for Giving

They say that it is better to give than to receive. The jury is out on this where cookies are concerned, when the joy of giving might be surpassed by the delight of eating. However, here are a variety of gift suggestions ranging from ideas for birthdays and congratulations to the most perfect hostess gift.

The simple Number Cookies, Vanilla Cream Cheese Cutouts and Wedding Bells are all pressed cookies and a great source of fun. There is such a fantastic range of cutters on the market that there is bound to be something that will appeal to everyone and be suited to every occasion. Let your imagination run wild with the decorations. Gather a collection of sprinkles, sugar flowers and coloured icings so that you can give your creativity free rein.

Buying presents for men can be challenging; make cookies instead. They will love the spicy flavours of the Cardamom Crisps, enjoy dipping the Pine Nut Biscotti in their coffee and find the Double Chocolate Mint Sandwiches irresistible.

For a sophisticated gift make the Pink and White Meringues or the Shortcake with a Hint of Rose. Wrap in delicate pink tissue and package in a clear bag tied with a trailing ribbon, in a classic presentation box, or even in a beautiful glass gift canister.

Number Cookies

If you can't find number cutters, trace some numbers, cut them out and use them as templates.

Preparation time: 35 minutes
Cooking time: 15 minutes

150g plain flour, sifted
55g ground almonds
115g lightly salted butter, cut into small pieces
1 egg yolk

175g chopped glacé pineapple decoration
225g ready-to-use decorator's icing
food colourings
1 tbsp apricot jam, warmed

Preheat oven to 180°C (gas mark 4). Grease several baking trays or line with nonstick baking parchment.

Put the flour and ground almonds in a mixing bowl and blend in the butter using your fingers until the mixture resembles fine bread crumbs. Stir in the egg yolk and chopped glacé pineapple and, using your hands, bring all the ingredients together to form a soft dough.

On a lightly floured surface, roll out the dough to about 5mm thick and stamp out squares using a 8cm cutter. Put on the baking trays and re-roll the trimmings as necessary. Prick the squares with a fork. Bake the cookies for 15 minutes or until lightly golden at the edges. Transfer to a wire rack to cool.

To decorate the cookies, put the icing in a bowl and add a few drops of colouring. Knead the icing until soft and smooth. On a surface lightly sprinkled with icing sugar, roll out the icing and stamp out numbers as required.

Brush the apricot jam over the surface of each cookie to fix a number to each one. Any leftover trimmings from the icing can be cut into thin strips and used as lengths of 'ribbon' to wrap bundles of cookies together. Store in an airtight container.

Makes 11

Cassis Pink Cookies

These very elegant cookies are only for the grown ups! They are flavoured with crème de cassis liqueur for a distinct taste.

Preparation time: 40 minutes
Cooking time: 10–15 minutes

225g plain flour, sifted
90g icing sugar
140g butter, cut into small pieces
85g finely chopped blanched
  almonds
2 tbsp crème de cassis liqueur

Decoration
60g unsalted butter, softened
115g icing sugar, sifted
1 tbsp crème de cassis liqueur
225g marzipan
pink food colouring
1 tbsp raspberry jam, warmed

TIP

Kirsch liqueur (cherry brandy) can be used instead of crème de cassis or, if you want to make a non-alcoholic version, use a fruit syrup instead.

Preheat the oven to 180°C (gas mark 4). Grease several baking trays or line with nonstick baking parchment.

Put the flour and icing sugar in a mixing bowl and blend in the butter, using your fingers until the mixture resembles fine bread crumbs. Stir in the chopped almonds and crème de cassis and mix all the ingredients together to form a firm dough.

On a lightly floured surface, roll out the dough to about 5mm thick. Stamp out 30 circles using a 6cm fluted cutter. Re-roll the trimmings as necessary and lift onto the prepared baking trays. Bake the cookies for 10–15 minutes, or until just beginning to turn golden at the edges. Transfer to a wire rack to cool.

To decorate the cookies, first make the icing by beating together the butter and icing sugar in a bowl to give a fluffy consistency. Gradually beat in the crème de cassis. Set aside. Add a few drops of pink colouring to the marzipan in a small bowl and knead until soft and smooth. On a clean surface lightly sprinkled with icing sugar, roll out the marzipan quite thinly and stamp out 15 circles using a 6cm fluted cutter.

Brush 15 of the cookies with the warmed raspberry jam and put a circle of marzipan on top. This will become the top of the cookies. Using the butter icing as the filling, sandwich the cookies together using the marzipan cookie for the top and the plain cookie for the base.

Makes 15

Vanilla Cream Cheese Cutouts

These tender cookies are perfect with just a simple sugar and nut topping.

Preparation time: 20 minutes + 1 hour chilling
Cooking time: 12–15 minutes

115g butter, softened
85g full-fat cream cheese
115g plain flour
200g icing sugar
1 tsp vanilla essence

Topping
1 tbsp sugar
1 tsp ground cinnamon
2 tbsp finely chopped almonds
1 egg

Beat together the butter and cream cheese in a bowl until creamy. Add the flour, sugar and vanilla essence and mix to form a soft dough. Wrap the dough in cling film and refrigerate until firm, about 1 hour.

Line two baking trays with nonstick baking parchment. On a lightly floured surface roll half the dough to 3mm thick (keep remaining dough refrigerated). Using a floured 5cm cutter, cut out as many cookies as possible. Arrange 2cm apart on the baking trays. Repeat with remaining dough and trimmings. Chill.

Preheat oven to 180°C (gas mark 4). For the topping stir together the sugar, cinnamon and almonds. In a separate bowl, lightly beat the egg with 1 tablespoon cold water. Brush the tops of the cookies with the egg and sprinkle with a little of the sugar-nut mixture. Bake for 12–15 minutes until golden. Transfer to a wire rack to cool.

Makes about 36

> **TIP**
>
> These are great basic cookies and can be cut to any shape. For kids' parties replace the spicy nut topping with coloured sugar or sprinkles.

Raspberry Meringues

These pastel meringues, which are as light as air and melt in the mouth, can be made up to a week in advance, and are fantastic for any celebration.

Preparation time: 30 minutes
Cooking time: 1 hour and 30 minutes

4 egg whites
pinch of salt
200g caster sugar
2 tbsp raspberry syrup

Preheat oven to 120°C (gas mark ½). Line several baking trays with nonstick baking parchment.

In a large clean bowl, using a balloon whisk or handheld electric mixer, whisk together the egg whites and salt until they form stiff peaks. Whisk in the sugar a little at a time; the meringue should start to look glossy. Continue whisking in the sugar until it has all been incorporated and the meringue is thick, shiny and stands in stiff peaks. Add the raspberry syrup and mix well.

Fill a piping bag with the meringue mixture. Using a 2cm star nozzle, pipe about 40 small whirls onto the baking trays.

Bake the meringues for 1 hour and 30 minutes, or until they are dry and crisp and can be easily lifted off the paper. Leave to cool completely.

Store unfilled meringues in an airtight container for up to a week.

Makes 40

TIP

Cold eggs separate more easily because the egg whites hold together better, but bring them up to room temperature for beating so that they are able to hold more air bubbles.

Maple Syrup Tuiles

Store these very delicate Mother's Day cookies carefully in an airtight container.

Preparation time: 25 minutes
Cooking time: 8–10 minutes

60g lightly salted butter
90g caster sugar
2 tbsp chopped almonds
3 tbsp maple syrup
55g plain flour, sifted

Preheat oven to 180°C (gas mark 4). Line two or three baking trays with nonstick baking parchment.

In a saucepan, gently heat the butter, caster sugar, almonds and maple syrup until the butter has melted. Remove from the heat. Add the flour and mix together until thoroughly blended.

Spoon four teaspoonfuls of the mixture well apart on the baking trays. Bake for 8–10 minutes until bubbly and the cookies have spread to a lacy texture. Remove from the oven, leave to cool for one minute then lift off with a thin metal spatula and curl around a rolling pin to mould into tuile shapes.

Shape the remaining cookies in the same way, and leave to go cold and crisp. Handle the tuiles very carefully once baked.

Makes about 21

TIP

If the tuiles have hardened before you have shaped them, pop them back in the oven for a few seconds to soften them.

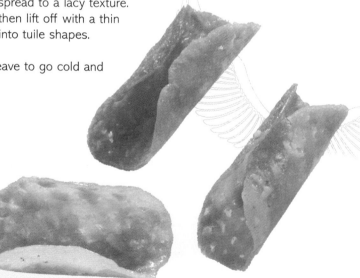

Shortcake with a Hint of Rose

These thick rounds of delicate shortcake have been flavoured with rose water.

TIP

Instead of raw sugar, sprinkle with pink coloured sugar.

Preparation time: 25 minutes
Cooking time: 25–30 minutes

170g plain flour, sifted
85g butter, cut into small pieces
70g caster sugar
1 egg yolk
2 tbsp rose water
raw sugar for sprinkling, optional

Preheat oven to 150˚C (gas mark 2). Grease several baking trays or line with nonstick baking parchment.

Put the flour in a mixing bowl and blend in the butter using your fingertips until the mixture resembles fine bread crumbs. Stir in the sugar, egg yolk and rose water, then bring everything together with your hands to form a soft dough. On a lightly floured surface, roll out the dough to about 5mm thick and using an 8cm cutter, stamp out rounds, lift onto the baking trays and prick with a fork. Repeat as necessary.

Sprinkle with raw sugar and bake the cookies for 25–30 minutes or until lightly golden. Transfer to a wire rack to cool.

Makes 10

Orange Flower Cookies

These pretty cookies, sandwiched together with an orange butter cream, are perfect for a Mother's Day tea.

Preparation time: 35 minutes + 30 minutes chilling
Cooking time: 15 minutes

175g lightly salted butter, softened
90g icing sugar, sifted
zest of 1 orange
200g plain flour, sifted
55g custard powder or cornflour
½ tsp vanilla essence

Filling
85g unsalted butter, softened
170g icing sugar, sifted
1 tsp orange zest
2 tsp fresh orange juice
icing sugar, for dusting

In a mixing bowl, beat together the butter and icing sugar until light and fluffy. Stir in the orange zest, flour, custard powder or cornflour, and vanilla and combine all the ingredients well. Using your hands, bring the mixture together to form a soft ball. Wrap and chill for 30 minutes.

Preheat oven to 180°C (gas mark 4). Grease several baking trays or line with nonstick baking parchment.

On a lightly floured work surface, roll out the dough to about 5mm thick. Using 5cm cutters, stamp out 13 flower shapes and 13 circles and transfer to the baking trays. Bake the cookies for 15 minutes, or until lightly golden brown and transfer to a wire rack to cool.

To decorate the cookies, in a small bowl beat together the butter and icing sugar until soft and stir in the orange zest and juice for a soft icing. Sandwich the flower shapes and the rounds together with butter cream and dust with icing sugar before serving. Store in an airtight container for up to one week.

Makes 13

Chocolate Macaroons

Show how much you care by presenting these classic cookies, enhanced by the addition of chocolate, to anyone you love.

Preparation time: 25 minutes
Cooking time: 25 minutes

85g egg whites (equal to whites of 3 large eggs), at room temperature
125g ground almonds
125g icing sugar
30g unsweetened cocoa powder
125g caster sugar, divided into two equal portions
125g dark chocolate
100 ml double cream
30g unsalted butter

> **TIP**
> Be careful when separating the eggs – just the tiniest speck of egg yolk will prevent the whites from bulking up properly.

Line two baking trays with parchment paper. Sift the ground almonds, icing sugar and cocoa powder into a large bowl. Place the egg whites in a separate bowl and add half of the caster sugar, and beat to stiff-peak consistency. Add the rest of the caster sugar and beat until all the sugar is dissolved. Fold the beaten egg whites into the almond mix, until incorporated. The batter should be smooth and glossy. Fit a large pastry bag with a 1cm tip, fill with the batter and pipe the mixture into small mounds about the size of walnuts. The batter should be fluid enough that the macaroons slowly flatten themselves out. Tap the trays against a hard surface a couple of times to remove any large air bubbles. Preheat the oven to 170°C (gas mark 3). Place the macaroons in a cool, dry place for 20–30 minutes until a skin forms. Bake for 12–14 minutes, until cooked, with the characteristic 'foot' underneath each macaroon.

To make the filling, heat the cream until nearly boiling, and then pour over the chocolate, stirring until melted. Allow to cool completely, stirring occasionally. Place 1 teaspoon chocolate-cream mixture on the underside of a macaroon, gently press another macaroon against the filling and carefully twist to spread. Refrigerate for 2 hours before serving. Store in an airtight container and consume within 2 days.

Makes 16

Valentine's Cookies

This two-tone dough creates a stunning effect, guaranteed to impress your Valentine!

Preparation time: 30 minutes + 30 minutes chilling
Cooking time: 15 minutes

175g butter, softened
90g icing sugar, sifted
½ tsp vanilla essence
250g plain flour, sifted
few drops of pink food colouring
granulated sugar, for sprinkling

In a mixing bowl beat together the butter and icing sugar until light and fluffy. Stir in the vanilla. Fold in the flour and bring all the ingredients together using your hands to form a soft dough. Take half the dough and add a few drops of colouring to turn the dough pink. Wrap the two doughs separately and chill for 30 minutes.

Preheat oven to 180°C (gas mark 4). Grease several baking trays or line with nonstick baking parchment.

On a lightly floured work surface, roll out each dough to about 5mm thick. Using a 5cm and 3cm heart-shaped cutter, stamp out hearts from both doughs and lift onto the baking trays. Re-position the centres to alternate the colours. Sprinkle with the granulated sugar. Bake the cookies for 15 minutes or until lightly golden. Allow to cool on the baking trays, before transferring to a wire rack to cool completely. Store these cookies in an airtight container to keep fresh.

Makes 22

Wedding Bells

These cookies contain marzipan in the dough, which gives them an almond flavour that mixes well with the lemon.

Preparation time: 45 minutes
Cooking time: 10–15 minutes

115g white marzipan, cut into small pieces
115g lightly salted butter, softened
50g caster sugar
1 egg yolk
zest of 1 lemon
150g plain flour, sifted

Decoration
2 tbsp apricot jam
yellow food colouring
400g ready-to-use fondant icing
gold ribbons, optional

TIP

If the marzipan is too hard to beat into the butter, put it in the microwave on medium for 10 seconds until slightly softened. Do not allow it to become hot or it will not beat properly to a light consistency.

Preheat oven to 180˚C (gas mark 4). Grease several baking trays or line with nonstick baking parchment.

In a mixing bowl, beat together the marzipan, butter and sugar until light and fluffy. Beat in the egg yolk and lemon zest. Add the flour and bring the mixture together with your hands to form a soft dough. On a lightly floured surface, roll out the dough to 5mm thick, and stamp out bells using a 6cm bell-shaped cutter. Re-roll the trimmings and stamp out more bells and put onto the baking trays. Make a hole at the top of each cookie with a metal skewer if you want to tie the bells with ribbons.

Bake the cookies for 10–15 minutes or until golden brown. Transfer to a wire rack and leave to cool. Brush each cookie with warmed apricot jam.

Add a few drops of yellow colouring to the icing and knead until soft and smooth. On a surface lightly sprinkled with icing sugar, roll out the icing and stamp out 30 bells using the same bell-shaped cutter, re-rolling as necessary. Press a icing 'bell' onto each cookie and re-shape the hole with a metal skewer, if necessary.

Makes 30

72

Lemon Rings

These cookies are sandwiched together with a lemon butter icing to symbolise wedding rings.

Preparation time: 35 minutes
Cooking time: 10–15 minutes

85g butter, softened	**Icing**
90g caster sugar	60g unsalted butter,
1 egg, beaten	softened
225g self-raising flour	115g icing sugar
zest of 1 lemon	2 tsp lemon juice
2 tbsp lemon juice	1 tsp lemon zest

TIP

These are ideal to give to a bride on her hen night. Look out for wedding biscuit cutter sets if you want to ring the changes!

Preheat oven to 180°C (gas mark 4). Grease several baking trays or line with nonstick baking parchment.

In a mixing bowl, beat together the butter and sugar until light and fluffy. Beat in the egg. Fold in the flour, lemon zest and lemon juice and mix all the ingredients together to form a firm dough. On a lightly floured surface, roll out the dough to about 5mm thick. Using a 6cm and 3cm cutter, cut out rings from the dough, carefully removing the central circle, and lift onto the baking trays. Re-roll the trimmings as necessary. Bake the cookies for 10–15 minutes. Transfer to a wire rack to cool.

To assemble the cookies, in a mixing bowl beat together the butter and icing sugar to give a fluffy consistency. Gradually beat in the lemon juice and zest. Sandwich the rings together with the filling and dust with icing sugar before serving.

Makes 16

Pine Nut Biscotti

Pine nuts and ground cinnamon are used to flavour these classic Italian cookies. They are a perfect gift for a difficult-to-buy-for man.

Preparation time: 30 minutes
Cooking time: 40–45 minutes

1 egg
7 tbsp caster sugar
115g plain flour, sifted
½ tsp baking powder
1 tsp ground cinnamon
⅔ cup pine nuts
icing sugar, for dusting

TIP

Biscotti are hard and crisp, perfectly designed to be dipped in coffee. If you want to nibble yours instead, then simply reduce the second cooking time slightly.

Preheat oven to 180°C (gas mark 4). Grease a large baking tray or line with nonstick baking parchment.

In a mixing bowl, whisk together the egg and sugar with an electric handheld mixer until pale and thick (ribbons of mixture should leave a trail from the whisk as you lift it).

Fold in the flour, baking powder, cinnamon and pine nuts and mix everything together to form a soft dough. Turn out onto a lightly floured work surface and roll into a 23cm log. Transfer onto the prepared baking tray and flatten the dough until it is about 2cm thick.

Bake the dough for about 30 minutes or until golden and firm. Leave to cool for about 5 minutes. Transfer to a chopping board and, using a serrated bread knife, cut the log on the diagonal into 1cm slices. Lift onto the baking tray and cook for a further 10–15 minutes or until crisp.

Transfer to a wire rack to cool. Dust with icing sugar and store in an airtight container for up to one week.

Makes 13

Butter Viennese Fingers

These cookies can look very impressive. They are crisp on the outside, but have a melt-in-the-mouth texture.

Preparation time: 25 minutes
Cooking time: 10–15 minutes

175g butter, softened
3 tbsp icing sugar, sifted
170g plain flour, sifted

Decoration
55g plain chocolate, broken into pieces

TIP

If made with the star nozzle, these cookies look very attractive sandwiched together with a little vanilla or coffee butter icing.

Preheat oven to 180°C (gas mark 4). Grease several baking trays or line with nonstick baking parchment.

In a large mixing bowl, beat together the butter and icing sugar until very soft, about 5 minutes. Beat in the flour until thoroughly mixed and a soft consistency is achieved.

Using a piping bag fitted with a medium star nozzle, pipe 8cm finger shapes on the baking trays, or spread the mixture evenly and mark fingers. Bake for 10–15 minutes or until pale golden. Cut into fingers, if necessary, and transfer to a wire rack to cool.

To decorate the cookies, put the chocolate in a small bowl and put this over a saucepan of simmering water. Stir frequently until the chocolate has melted. Dip the ends of each cookie in the chocolate and leave to set on greaseproof paper or baking parchment.

Makes 20

Lime and Coconut Hearts

Exotic flavours of coconut and lime are reminiscent of the Caribbean.

Preparation time: 35 minutes
Cooking time: 15 minutes

225g plain flour, sifted
25g rice flour
175g butter, cut in pieces
90g caster sugar
75g dessicated coconut
zest of 1 lime
2 tbsp milk

Decoration
7 tbsp icing sugar, sifted
zest of 1 lime

TIP

Don't save these for Valentine's Day – they are a perfect 'goodbye' gift for someone going travelling.

Preheat oven to 180°C (gas mark 4). Grease several baking trays or line with nonstick baking parchment.

Put the flour and rice flour in a mixing bowl and add the butter. Blend in the butter using your fingers until the mixture resembles fine bread crumbs. Add the sugar, coconut, lime zest and milk and mix all the ingredients together to form a soft dough.

On a lightly floured work surface, roll out the dough to about 5mm. Stamp out hearts using a 8cm heart-shaped cutter and lift onto the baking trays. Bake for 15 minutes or until lightly golden. Transfer to a wire rack to cool.

To serve, dust with icing sugar and a touch of fresh lime zest. Store in an airtight container for up to three days.

Makes 16

Coffee Kisses

Sometimes, you have to say it with a kiss. For an extra-special touch, pipe a little melted chocolate in an 'x' shape on the top.

Preparation time: 25 minutes
Cooking time: 1 hour and 30 minutes

200g plain flour	**Filling**
1 tsp baking powder	60g butter, softened
85g butter	85g icing sugar
55g caster sugar	1 tsp cocoa powder
30g soft brown sugar	1 tbsp crème fraiche or thick
1 egg, beaten	yoghurt
2 tbsp strong black coffee	2–3 tsp strong black coffee

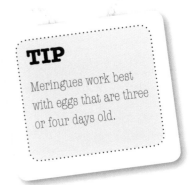

TIP
Meringues work best with eggs that are three or four days old.

Heat the oven to 180°C (gas mark 4). Line two baking sheets with baking parchment. Sift the flour and the baking powder into a large mixing bowl. Cut the butter into small pieces, add into the flour and rub in. Mix in the sugars. Add 1 tbsp of boiling water to the instant coffee and add to the mix, along with the egg. Mix well until it comes together into a sticky dough. Form into 24 balls the size of cherries. Place onto the baking sheets, 5cm apart, and flatten slightly. Bake for 15 minutes or until golden brown, and transfer to a wire rack to cool.

To make the filling: beat together the butter and icing sugar until light and fluffy. Add the cocoa powder, creme fraiche and coffee to taste. When the cookies are cold, sandwich them together with the butter cream.

Makes about 12

Cardamom Crisps

These indulgent and sophisticated cookies flavoured with cardamom are delicious. They will liven up anyone's nightcap.

Preparation time: 25 minutes
Cooking time: 15 minutes

250g plain flour, sifted
½ tsp ground cardamom (or fresh cardamom pods, see tip)
pinch of salt
115g lightly salted butter, cut into small pieces

225g soft brown sugar
2 egg yolks
fresh cardamom pods, to decorate

TIP

If using cardamom pods, crack open 7 pods, remove the black seeds and crush with a pestle and mortar.

Preheat oven to 180°C (gas mark 4). Grease several baking trays or line with nonstick baking parchment.

Put the flour, ground cardamom and salt in a mixing bowl. Blend in the butter, using your fingers, until the mixture resembles fine bread crumbs, then stir in the sugar. Add the egg yolks and mix all the ingredients together to form a soft dough.

With lightly floured hands, roll 20 small balls of dough, and place on prepared baking trays. Place a fresh cardamom seed on top of each cookie. Bake the cookies for 15 minutes or until lightly golden and crisp. Transfer the cookies to a wire rack and leave to cool. Store in an airtight container for up to two weeks.

Makes about 20

Double Chocolate Mint Sandwiches

A delicious combination of mint-flavoured white chocolate ganache sandwiched between thin cocoa wafers. Perfect to say thank you for a dinner invitation.

Preparation time: 1 hour + chilling
Cooking time: 12–16 minutes

115g plain flour
90g unsweetened cocoa powder
115g butter
50g caster sugar
1 egg

120ml whipping cream
200g quality white chocolate, chopped
1 tsp mint essence

Glaze
140g plain chocolate, chopped
85g butter, cut into pieces

TIP

For an even more decadent cookie, swirl a circle of melted bitter chocolate on one wafer. Allow to set for another hour or so in a cool place before serving.

Filling

Sift the flour and cocoa. In a large bowl, beat the butter until creamy, add the sugar, then beat until light and fluffy. Beat in the egg until blended. Stir in the flour-cocoa mixture to form a soft dough. Put this in cling film and refrigerate for 1–2 hours until firm.

Preheat oven to 180°C (gas mark 4). Grease two baking trays with nonstick baking parchment.

On a lightly floured work surface, roll out half the dough to about 3mm thick. Cut out cookies using a 6cm cutter. Bake for 6–8 minutes or until the edges are set. Allow to cool and then transfer to a wire rack to cool completely. Repeat with the remaining dough.

In a medium saucepan over a medium heat, bring the cream to the boil. Remove from the heat and add the white chocoate, stirring until melted. Stir in mint essence and strain into a bowl. Cool until firm. Slightly beat the cream, then use this to sandwich the cookies together.

Refrigerate until set, then store in an airtight container, refrigerated, for up to two days.

Makes about 24

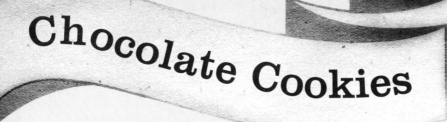

Chocolate Cookies

Could there be anything more divine than a sumptuous chocolate-flavoured cookie? All that decadence in an oh-so-easy-to-eat morsel. Heaven on earth, surely.

Chocolate Cookies

Few of us can resist the temptation of an enticing chocolate cookie. Home-baked chocolate cookies bring back memories of childhood. The aroma of chocolate baking in the oven, the pile of delectable cookies on the cooking rack and time passing slowly waiting for them to be cool. If the smell didn't get you at home, then it sure did as you passed the bakery.

Chocolate offers so much variety: rich velvety dark chocolate versus creamy milky chocolate, versus vanilla-scented, smooth white chocolate. Do you fancy a cookie studded with little nuggets of chocolate, or a rich smooth texture with all-through flavour? Is your dream cookie soft and gooey or crisp and snappy? Frosted or unfrosted? Filled or unfilled? In this chapter we have selected some gems to satisfy all your chocolate desires.

If it is simplicity you desire then nothing could be nicer than the Chocolate Crackle-Tops, which along with the Ultimate Chocolate Chip Cookie will become cookie jar staples. There's some fantastic party cookies, the Red, White and Blue Cookies, the Chocolate Frosted Heart Cookies and Pinwheel Cookies, to mention a few. There are some chocoholic dessert cookies too – for instance, serve the Chocolate Wafers with a nutty ice cream and you can be certain you won't be bothered with leftovers!

Honeycomb–chocolate Crunchies

This is a small crunchy cookie, perfect for a lunchbox or picnic.

Preparation time: 20 minutes
Cooking time: 15 minutes

170g plain flour
85g slightly salted butter, softened
115g light brown sugar
1 egg
85g plain chocolate, chopped
85g honeycomb pieces

Preheat oven to 180°C (gas mark 4). Grease two baking trays or line with nonstick baking parchment.

Sift the flour into a bowl. Beat together the butter and sugar in a separate bowl. Beat in the egg. Mix the sifted flour into the butter with the chocolate and honeycomb pieces.

Mold the mixture into 24 pieces. Put on baking trays and press the top lightly with a fork. Bake for 15 minutes. Leave to cool on the baking tray. Store in an airtight container.

Makes about 24

TIP

For a double dose of chocolate, scatter plain or white chocolate chips over the hot cookies, then press down lightly to melt the base of the chocolate into the cookie to stick. Let cool.

Chequerboards

These cookies are good fun to make and look impressive for children's parties.

Preparation time: 25 minutes + 1 hour chilling
Cooking time: 15–20 minutes

170g butter, softened	500g plain flour
150g caster sugar	2 tsp baking powder
½ tsp vanilla essence	1 tsp milk
2 eggs	1½ tbsp unsweetened cocoa powder, sifted

Divide the butter and sugar evenly between 2 bowls. For the vanilla dough, beat butter and sugar together until light and fluffy. Beat in the vanilla essence and one egg. Sift half the flour and baking powder into the bowl. Blend in with a spoon and then work by hand to form a smooth dough.

Make the chocolate dough in the same way with the remaining butter, sugar and egg, adding milk and sifted cocoa along with the remaining flour and baking powder. Divide each portion of dough into 4 equal pieces.

On a floured surface roll each piece into a rope 30cm long. Put a chocolate rope next to a vanilla one. Put a chocolate one on top of the vanilla rope and a vanilla one on top of the chocolate. Press firmly together to form a square. Wrap in cling film. Repeat with remaining dough. Chill for 1 hour in the refrigerator.

Preheat oven to 180°C (gas mark 4). Grease two baking trays or line with nonstick baking parchment.

Cut dough into 26 slices and put onto the baking trays. Bake for 15–20 minutes until lightly browned. Transfer to a wire rack to cool. Once completely cool, store in an airtight container.

Makes about 26

TIP

Instead of chequerboards, twist two chocolate dough ropes and two vanilla dough ropes together and roll into a smooth thick rope. Chill and cut into slices to cook.

Chocolate Crackle-Tops

A simple chocolate cookie which is easy to make and will become a family favourite.

Preparation time: 25 minutes + 1 hour chilling
Cooking time: 10–15 minutes

200g plain chocolate, chopped
85g slightly salted butter, softened
90g caster sugar
3 eggs
1 tsp vanilla essence
170g plain flour

25g unsweetened cocoa
  powder
½ tsp baking powder
170g icing sugar, for
  decoration

Heat the chocolate and butter in a saucepan over a low heat, stirring frequently. Remove from the heat and stir in the sugar. Continue stirring for 2–3 minutes until the sugar dissolves. Add the eggs one at a time, beating well. Add vanilla.

Sift the flour, cocoa and baking powder into a bowl. Gradually stir into the chocolate mixture in batches, until just blended. Cover dough and refrigerate for 1 hour or until cold.

Preheat oven to 160˚C (gas mark 3). Grease two baking trays or line with nonstick baking parchment.

Put icing sugar in a small bowl. Using a teaspoon, scoop dough into small balls and between palms of hand, roll into 1cm balls. Drop balls one at a time into icing sugar and roll until heavily coated. Remove balls with a slotted spoon and tap against the side of the bowl to remove excess sugar.

Put the cookies on baking trays spaced well apart. Bake for 10–15 minutes. Leave to cool on baking tray for 3 minutes then remove to wire cooling rack. Eat within 2 days.

Makes about 48

Oat Jacks

A perfect lunchbox treat or a substantial afternoon snack. Try dipping them in white chocolate too.

Preparation time: 15 minutes
Cooking time: 25–30 minutes

115g slightly salted butter, softened
170g white chocolate
115g light brown sugar
170g rolled oats

Preheat oven to 160°C (gas mark 3). Grease or line a shallow 20 x 20cm tin with nonstick baking parchment.

Melt the butter and white chocolate over a medium heat in a saucepan, then transfer to a bowl. Stir in the sugar and rolled oats.

Spoon the mixture into the baking tin and bake for 25–30 minutes. Leave to cool in the tin for 5 minutes, then cut into squares.

Makes 12

TIP

For an even more decadent oat jack, melt 170g milk chocolate, and use to coat the squares.

Spiced Rum Chocolate Cookies

A small, dark and sophisticated chocolate cookie: strictly for the adults.

Preparation time: 20 minutes
Cooking time: 10–12 minutes

170g light brown sugar
2 eggs, separated
170g plain flour
1 tbsp unsweetened cocoa powder
1 tsp ground cinnamon
1 tsp mixed spice
70g caster sugar
zest of ½ orange
2 tbsp rum

TIP

Use orange juice instead of rum for a non-alcholic version of these cookies.

Preheat oven to 190˚C (gas mark 5). Grease two baking trays or line with nonstick baking parchment.

Beat together the brown sugar with the egg yolks until light and fluffy. Sift the flour and spices together, then stir in until the mixture resembles bread crumbs. Whisk the egg whites until they form stiff peaks and then beat in the caster sugar until glossy. Fold into the mixture with the orange zest.

Roll the mixture into walnut-sized pieces and put onto the baking trays. Bake for 10–15 minutes. Brush with rum while still warm, then use a metal spatula to transfer to a wire cooling rack to cool completely. Store in an airtight container.

Makes about 18

Chocolate Pinwheels

A good, fun cookie, that is great for kid's parties.

Preparation time: 25 minutes + up to 2 hours chilling
Cooking time: 8–10 minutes

115g slightly salted butter, softened
70g caster sugar
1 egg, beaten
1 tsp vanilla essence

150g plain flour
pinch of salt
30g plain chocolate

In a large bowl beat together the butter and sugar until light and fluffy. Beat in the egg and vanilla until blended. Sift the flour and salt onto the mixture and beat briefly until combined.

Divide the dough in half and wrap one half in cling film. Refrigerate until firm enough to roll. Melt the chocolate in a small bowl set over a saucepan of simmering water. Let cool slightly. Add the melted chocolate to the remaining dough and mix until completely blended. Wrap chocolate dough in cling film and refrigerate until firm enough to roll.

On a lightly floured surface or between 2 sheets of cling film, roll the vanilla dough to a rectangle. Repeat with the chocolate dough, rolling to the same size. If rolling between sheets of film, remove top sheet and put chocolate dough on top of plain dough. Roll up dough from one short end as tightly as possible. Wrap tightly and refrigerate until very firm.

Preheat oven to 190°C (gas mark 5). Grease two baking trays or line with nonstick baking parchment.

Using a sharp knife, cut the dough roll into 5mm slices and set well apart onto the baking trays. Bake for 7–10 minutes, until beginning to change colour at the edges. Transfer to a wire rack and once completely cool, store in an airtight container.

Makes about 25

> **TIP**
> The initial beating together of the butter and sugar is best done using an electric mixer. Beat for between 1 and 2 minutes, until light and fluffy. Reduce the speed to low to add any dry ingredients.

Mocha Chunk Cookies

These are seriously good adult cookies. They make a great offering for any celebration.

Preparation time: 20 minutes
Cooking time: 20 minutes

150g plain flour
2 tbsp unsweetened cocoa powder
¼ tsp bicarbonate of soda
pinch of salt
2 tsp instant coffee granules
1 tsp coffee liqueur, optional
90g caster sugar
55g packed dark brown sugar
115g slightly salted butter, softened
1 egg
2 cups plain chocolate, coarsely chopped

> **TIP**
>
> Softened butter will leave a deep indentation when pressed with a finger, but is still firm enough to pick up without falling apart.

Preheat oven to 180˚C (gas mark 4). Grease two baking trays or line with nonstick baking parchment.

Into a medium-sized bowl, sift the flour, cocoa, bicarbonate of soda and salt. In a small bowl dissolve coffee granules in coffee liqueur or hot water and set aside. In a large bowl, mix together the sugars. Add the butter and beat thoroughly until light. Add the eggs and coffee mixture and beat until smooth. Add the flour mixture and the chocolate chunks and mix gently with a spoon until well combined.

Put rounded tablespoons of the mixture onto the baking trays spaced 5cm apart. Bake for 20 minutes until set. Transfer cookies to a flat surface to cool. Once completely cool, store in an airtight container.

Makes about 16

Chocolate-Fudge Drops

Crunchy and chewy on the outside, soft and gooey in the middle, these are so easy to make, and so easy to eat!

Preparation time: 15 minutes + 1 hour chilling
Cooking time: 8–10 minutes

1½ cup plain chocolate chips
40g + 1 tbsp butter
2 eggs
150g sugar
4 tbsp flour
½ tsp baking powder
1 tsp salt

In a large saucepan, melt the butter and chocolate chips and mix in the sugar, stirring until dissolved. Allow to cool a little, before beating in the eggs. Add the flour, baking powder and salt and mix to combine.

Allow mixture to firm up in a cool place for at least an hour. Preheat oven to 180°C (gas mark 4). Grease two baking trays or line with nonstick baking parchment. Using a small ice cream scoop, place balls of the mixture on the prepared baking sheets.

Bake for 8–10 minutes, until the outsides of the cookies are just cooked. The insides will be a little soft, like a good brownie. Transfer to a wire rack to cool completely. Store in an airtight container for up to a week, or freeze for up to 3 months.

Makes about 30

TIP

Turn the baking tray around halfway through cooking if your oven does not cook evenly.

Ultimate Chocolate Chip Cookies

Huge cookies, the ultimate indulgence, a cookie packed with three types of chocolate. Make these as large as you dare.

Preparation time: 20 minutes
Cooking time: 18–20 minutes

170g flour
½ tsp baking powder
pinch of salt
115g slightly salted butter,
  softened
115g light brown sugar
½ tbsp honey

1 egg
1 tsp vanilla essence
½ cup plain chocolate chips
½ cup milk chocolate chips
½ cup white chocolate chips

TIP

This recipe can be used to make 6 giant coffee-shop-sized cookies.

Preheat oven to 160˚C (gas mark 3). Grease two baking trays or line with nonstick baking parchment.

Sift the flour, baking powder and salt together into a bowl. Beat together the softened butter and light brown sugar until light and fluffy. Gradually beat in the egg, vanilla and honey. Stir in the flour mixture and all of the chocolate. Mix all the ingredients together until they are just combined.

Drop about 2 tablespoonfuls of the dough spaced 5–8cm apart on baking trays. Bake the cookies for 18–22 minutes, depending on their size. Transfer them to a wire rack to cool. Once completely cool, store in an airtight container.

Makes 10–12

Chocolate Ginger Cookies

Ginger preserve gives a lovely flavour without the harshness sometimes associated with ground ginger.

Preparation time: 25 minutes
Cooking time: 18–20 minutes

115g packed dark brown sugar
50g caster sugar
115g slightly salted butter, softened
1 egg
1 tsp ginger or golden syrup
170g plain flour
½ tsp baking powder
pinch of salt
½ cup plain chocolate chips
⅓ cup ginger preserve

TIP

To make ginger syrup, combine ¾ cup sliced unpeeled ginger, 200g (7oz) of sugar and 450ml of water in a saucepan. Slowly bring to a boil and simmer for 10 minutes. Cool to room temperature and strain. It's great with sparkling water.

Preheat oven to 150°C (gas mark 2). Grease two baking trays or line with nonstick baking parchment.

In a large bowl blend the sugars together. Add the butter and beat together until light. Add the egg and ginger or golden syrup and mix well. Sift the flour, baking powder and salt into the mixture. Add the chocolate chips and ginger preserve and mix thoroughly with a spoon.

Drop rounded tablespoons onto a baking tray spaced 5cm apart. Bake the cookies for 18–20 minutes or until golden brown. Transfer cookies to a flat surface and cool completely. Store in an airtight container.

Makes about 20

Red, White and Blue Cookies

The perfect 4th July cookie. Dried sour cherries and blueberries make a lovely sweet–sour contrast to the sweet white chocolate.

TIP

If you haven't got dried sour cherries, use dried cranberries instead.

Preparation time: 20 minutes
Cooking time: 8–10 minutes

115g plain flour
25g unsweetened cocoa powder
1 tsp baking powder
pinch of salt
115g slightly salted butter, softened
200g granulated sugar
1 egg
½ tsp vanilla essence
1 cup white chocolate chips
30g roughly chopped dried sour cherries
30g dried blueberries

Preheat oven to 180°C (gas mark 4). Grease two baking trays or line with nonstick baking parchment.

Sift the flour, cocoa, baking powder and salt into a medium bowl. Beat together the butter and sugar in a large bowl until light and fluffy. Beat in the egg and vanilla until blended. Beat in the flour mixture at low speed until just combined. Stir in the chocolate chips, sour cherries and blueberries.

Drop rounded teaspoonfuls of the dough onto the baking trays. Bake for 8–10 minutes, until just firm. Transfer to a wire rack to cool. Once completely cool, store in airtight container.

Makes about 36

Black-and-White Sandwich Cookies

Are you a twister or a dunker? Make your mind up with these homemade classic cookies.

TIP

To make chocolate-mint sandwiches, substitute mint essence for the vanilla essence.

Preparation time: 45 minutes + 2 hours chilling
Cooking time: 8 minutes

90g plain flour, plus more for dusting
40g cocoa powder
85g unsalted butter, softened
90g icing sugar, sifted
1 large egg
½ teaspoon pure vanilla essence

For the filling
1 egg white
50g sugar
2 tbsp golden syrup
1 tbsp water
½ tsp vanilla essence

Sift the flour and cocoa into a bowl. In a separate large bowl, beat the butter and sugar together until light and fluffy. Gradually beat in the egg and vanilla essence until well combined; stir in the flour-cocoa mixture. Spoon the dough into a piece of cling film and shape into a flat disc. Wrap well and refrigerate for 2 hours or overnight until firm.

Preheat oven to 180°C (gas mark 4). Grease two baking trays or line with nonstick baking parchment. On a lightly floured surface roll out half of the cookie dough as thin as possible. Using a 4cm cutter, cut out as many cookies as possible. Re-roll and cut out trimmings. Bake the cookies for 6–8 minutes until set. Cool on a wire rack and then repeat the process with the remaining dough.

To make the filling, whisk the egg white to stiff peaks in a heatproof bowl. In a medium saucepan, heat the sugar, golden syrup and water to 116°C (use a sugar thermometer). Remove from heat and pour the hot sugar syrup in a thin stream into the egg white, whisking constantly. Beat until thick and very glossy. Use a piping bag to pipe filling onto the centre of the base of a cookie, and gently press cookies together to push filling to edges.

Makes about 25

Orange & Chocolate-Chip Shortbread

A cookie classic, brought right up to date with the addition of zesty orange flavour.

Preparation time: 20 minutes

60g butter
200g caster sugar
1 egg, beaten
1 tsp orange essence
315g plain flour
25g unsweetened cocoa powder
2 tbsp cornflour
⅓ cup plain chocolate chips
zest of 1 orange

TIP
These cookies freeze very well for up to 3 months, either as dough or as baked cookies.

Preheat oven to 180°C (gas mark 4). Lightly grease two baking trays or line with nonstick baking parchment.

Beat the butter and sugar until light and fluffy. Gradually add the egg. Sift the flour and cocoa with the cornflour and work into the butter mixture with the chocolate chips to make a stiff dough. Lightly knead the dough for a few seconds until smooth.

Roll out on a floured surface to a thickness of 5mm. Cut into 20 with a plain or fluted 8cm cutter. Bake in the oven for 15 minutes, until firm to the touch. Leave the cookies to cool on the baking trays for a few minutes, then remove to a wire rack to cool completely.

Makes about 26

Chocolate-coated Gingerbread

An understated Valentine or birthday cookie, perfect with coffee.

Preparation time: 1 hour + 1 hour
   chilling
Cooking time: 8–10 minutes

115g slightly salted butter, softened
75g brown sugar
150ml molasses
1 tsp ground ginger
1 tsp cinnamon
½ tsp ground cloves

1 tsp bicarbonate of soda
1 egg, beaten
450g plain flour
225g plain chocolate chips

TIP

These would look very sophisticated decorated with chopped pistachio nuts.

Preheat oven to 160˚C (gas mark 3). Grease two baking trays or line with nonstick baking parchment.

Cut the butter into pieces and put in a large bowl. Put the sugar, molasses and spices in a saucepan and bring to the boil. Add the bicarbonate of soda and pour into the bowl with the butter. Stir until the butter has melted, then stir in the egg. Sift in the flour and mix until thoroughly combined. Chill the dough until firm enough to roll out.

Roll out 5mm thick on a lightly floured surface. Cut out circles with a 8cm cutter. Put onto the baking trays and bake in batches for 8–10 minutes. Transfer to a wire rack to cool completely.

Melt the chocolate chips and dip half of each cookie in the chocolate. Return the cookies to wire rack to set. Once set, store in an airtight container for up to a week.

Makes about 45

Chocolate Wafers

These nutty thins are great served with ice cream.

Preparation time: 20 minutes
Cooking time: 15 minutes

115g slightly salted butter, softened
90g caster sugar
120ml golden syrup
1 egg
½ tsp vanilla essence
115g plain flour
1 tbsp unsweetened cocoa powder
¼ tsp bicarbonate of soda
¾ cup chopped mixed nuts

TIP

If cooking in batches, allow the baking trays to return to room temperature in between uses.

Preheat oven to 180°C (gas mark 4). Line two baking trays with nonstick baking parchment.

Beat the butter, sugar and syrup together until light and fluffy. Thoroughly beat in the egg and vanilla. Sift the flour, cocoa and bicarbonate of soda onto the butter mixture. Lightly stir into the mixture with the chopped mixed nuts.

Put walnut-sized spoonfuls spaced 5cm apart onto the baking trays. Bake for 15 minutes. Lift from the baking tray with a thin metal spatula and lay over a lightly oiled rolling pin to produce a curved shape. Leave to cool on the rolling pin for a few minutes before transferring to a wire rack to cool completely. Once completely cool, store in an airtight container.

Makes about 28

Chocolate Viennese Whirls

A rich and attractive cookie, great for a smart afternoon tea party.

Preparation time: 25 minutes
Cooking time: 20 minutes

170g butter
55g icing sugar
170g plain flour
½ tsp vanilla essence
10 candied cherries, halved
170g plain chocolate, coarsely chopped

TIP

Replace 2 tablespoons of flour with 2 tablespoons sifted unsweetened cocoa powder, if you prefer your cookies to be chocolaty too.

Preheat oven to 160°C (gas mark 3). Grease two baking trays or line with nonstick baking parchment.

Beat together the butter and sugar until light and fluffy. Sift the flour into the bowl, add the vanilla and mix well to combine.

Spoon the mixture into a piping bag fitted with a large star-shaped nozzle. Pipe flat whirls onto the baking trays. Put half a cherry on each one. Bake for 20 minutes until just golden. Leave to cool on the baking tray for 5 minutes then transfer to a wire rack to cool completely.

Meanwhile, melt the chocolate in a small bowl set over a saucepan of simmering water. When the cookies are cold, dip into the melted chocolate. Put on a sheet of greaseproof paper until the chocolate has set, then store in an airtight container.

Makes about 20

Raspberry & White Chocolate Chunkies

A sweet and fruity cookie, great served with vanilla ice cream.

Preparation time: 20 minutes
Cooking time: 20 minutes

170g plain flour
¼ tsp bicarbonate of soda
pinch of salt
140g caster sugar
115g slightly salted butter, softened
1 tbsp beaten egg
⅓ cup sieved raspberry jam
170g white chocolate, coarsely chopped

TIP

If your cookies seem to spread too much, make sure that you are not over-greasing the baking trays.

Preheat oven to 150˚C (gas mark 2). Grease two baking trays or line with nonstick baking parchment.

Sift the flour, bicarbonate of soda and salt and set aside. Beat together the sugar and butter until light and fluffy. Beat in the egg and then the raspberry jam. Add the flour mixture and white chocolate chunks and mix to combine.

Drop tablespoonfuls onto the baking trays spaced about 5cm apart. Bake for 20 minutes. Transfer to a cool surface. When cold, store in an airtight container.

Makes about 16

Chocolate Mint Cookies

. . . .

A nice late-in-the-day cookie.

Preparation time: 20 minutes
Cooking time: 20 minutes

170g plain flour
¼ tsp baking powder
pinch of salt
25g unsweetened cocoa powder
75g light brown sugar
70g granulated sugar

115g slightly salted butter,
  softened
1 egg
1 tsp mint essence
⅔ cup plain chocolate chips

TIP

You can buy gourmet mint chocolate chips, which would be delicious in this recipe. Alternatively make your own from a bar of chocolate.

Preheat oven to 150˚C (gas mark 2). Grease two baking trays or line with nonstick baking parchment.

Sift the flour, baking powder, salt and cocoa into a bowl and set aside. In a separate bowl, beat together the sugars and butter until light. Beat in the eggs and mint essence until thoroughly blended. Add the flour mixture and chocolate chips, and mix well to combine. Do not over-mix.

Drop rounded tablespoonfuls of the mixture onto the baking trays spaced 4cm apart. Bake for 20 minutes until lightly golden. Transfer to a cool flat surface. When completely cool, store in an airtight container.

Makes about 18

Chocolate Rugelach

A traditional Jewish cookie much loved by children.

Preparation time: 45 minutes + 1-2 hours chilling
Cooking time: 20 minutes

225g strong flour
pinch of salt
115g slightly salted butter, softened
115g cream cheese
¼ cup sour cream
3 tbsp caster sugar
1 egg, separated
⅔ cup apricot jam
90g plain chocolate, finely chopped
2 tbsp caster sugar

TIP

Instead of sprinkling the apricot jam with chopped chocolate, use the same quantity of chopped pecans.

Sift the flour and salt into a large bowl. Put the flour with the butter, cream cheese, sour cream, sugar and egg yolk in a food processor. Process until a soft dough forms. Shape dough into a ball and flatten into a disc. Wrap in cling film and refrigerate for 1–2 hours.

Preheat oven to 180°C (gas mark 4). Grease two baking trays or line with nonstick baking parchment.

On a lightly floured surface, roll out one quarter of the dough to 3mm thick. Using a plate as a guide, cut the dough into a 25cm circle. Spread with 3 tablespoons of apricot jam, leaving a small border around the edge. Sprinkle with the chopped chocolate.

Cut this round into 12 equal-sized wedges. Starting at the widest end, roll up each wedge Swiss roll-style. Put on the baking tray spaced 3cm apart. Beat the egg white with 1 tablespoon of water, and brush each roll with a little of the egg and water. Sprinkle each roll with a little sugar. Repeat with the remaining dough.

Bake until puffed and golden brown. Turn the baking tray around halfway through cooking. Cool on the baking tray for a few minutes then transfer to a wire cooling rack to cool completely.

Makes about 60

Cookies for Cherubs

Cherubs love their cookies – they adore eating them and have even more fun making them. What better way to spend time together than in a warm, welcoming kitchen painting wiggly lines on wonky cookies.

Cookies for Cherubs

The cookies in this chapter divide into those that are made for the delight of kids and those that kids delight in making. The former allow your creativity to shine through. Alphabet cookies spelling out the name of the birthday boy or the initials of each party guest are just so much fun to make. The child in us all is unleashed when given a palette of coloured icings and the blank canvas of naked gingerbread characters. Set aside plenty of time for these – you're sure to get absorbed.

There are a number of simpler cookies too, such as the Apple Cookies, the Jewelled Cookie Bars and the Fruit Segments, which children love to eat but that require no decorative skills.

Kids, of course, will spend hours making cookies for their own party, as a gift for grandma or a teacher, or just for a fun wet-weather activity. Have plenty of brightly coloured tubes of icing available for them to play with. Coloured sugar and sprinkles also come in a huge variety of shapes and forms. Small sweets are useful as decorations, as are liquorice laces in red and black. Make sure you have plenty, because much of it will disappear before it ever gets used to decorate the cookies.

Alphabet Cookies

These cookies have a bright lemon flavour, which just melts in the mouth.

Preparation time: 30 minutes
Cooking time: 15–20 minutes

60g butter, softened
70g caster sugar
1 egg yolk
170g plain flour, sifted
½ tsp baking powder

2 tbsp lemon juice
zest of ½ a lemon
1 tbsp milk
icing sugar,
    for dusting

Preheat oven to 170°C (gas mark 3). Grease two baking trays or line with nonstick baking parchment.

In a mixing bowl, beat together the butter and caster sugar until pale and fluffy, then add the egg yolk, flour, baking powder, lemon juice and lemon zest, blending everything together.

Add the milk and mix to a firm dough, using your hands so that the dough comes together in a soft ball. Turn the dough out onto a lightly floured work surface and divide into about 25 equal-sized pieces. Roll each piece into a sausage shape with your hands and make letters of the alphabet, twisting the dough and trimming with a small knife, as needed.

Put the cookies onto the baking trays and bake for 15–20 minutes. Lift them onto a wire rack to cool completely before dusting with icing sugar. Store in an airtight container for up to one week.

Makes about 25

Balloon Cookies

These cookies are thick and crunchy, and you can really taste the coconut and orange flavours.

Preparation time: 40 minutes + 30 minutes chilling
Cooking time: 15–20 minutes

60g butter, softened
90g caster sugar
1 egg, beaten
115g plus 2 tbsp self-raising flour
50g sweetened dessicated coconut
zest of 1 orange

Decoration
115g icing sugar, sifted
1 tbsp water
4 food colourings
coloured ribbons

In a mixing bowl, beat together the butter and sugar until pale and fluffy. Beat in the egg, sift in the flour and add the coconut and orange zest. Mix all the ingredients together with your hands until they come together in a soft ball. Chill the dough in cling film in the refrigerator for 30 minutes.

Preheat oven to 170°C (gas mark 3). Grease two baking trays or line with baking parchment.

On a lightly floured work surface, roll out the dough, keeping it quite thick. If cracks appear, gather up the dough, sprinkle more flour on the work surface and try again. Using a 6cm round cutter, cut out the cookies and lift onto the baking trays. Using a metal skewer, make a hole at the top of each cookie for the ribbon. Bake the cookies for 15–20 minutes or until lightly golden. As soon as they come out of the oven re-shape the holes with the skewer. Lift them onto a wire rack to cool.

To decorate the cookies, mix the icing sugar with sufficient water to form a thin icing. Divide into four bowls and colour each one using a few drops of food colour. Spread different colours onto each cookie and when the icing has set, tie ribbons through the holes.

Makes 16

Chocolate Chip Cookies

These are simple chocolate chip cookies at their best. They are easy to make, chewy and full of chocolate chunks in every bite.

Preparation time: 25 minutes
Cooking time: 10–12 minutes

115g butter, softened
280g light brown sugar
1 egg, beaten
115g plain flour, sifted
½ tsp bicarbonate of soda
1 tsp vanilla essence
½ cup plain chocolate chips

TIP

Make two batches. Flash freeze one batch, uncooked, on the baking trays. Once frozen, remove from the baking trays and pack in rigid containers. Cook from frozen, adding a couple of minutes to the cooking time.

Preheat oven to 190°C (gas mark 5). Grease several baking trays or line with nonstick baking parchment.

In a bowl, beat together the butter and sugar until light and fluffy. Beat in the egg, a little at a time. Stir in the flour, bicarbonate of soda and vanilla, then add the chocolate chips, stirring until evenly spread throughout the mixture.

Spoon mounds of the mixture onto the baking trays, spacing them well apart for spreading. Using the back of a fork, flatten the balls slightly. Bake the cookies for 10–12 minutes or until golden. Transfer to a wire rack to cool.

Makes 20

Chocolate Twinkles

The perfect reward for a good deed or report card, these will make any child feel special.

Preparation time: 35 minutes + 30 minutes chilling
Cooking time: 15 minutes

170g plain flour, sifted
85g butter, cut into small pieces
150g caster sugar

Decoration
225g milk chocolate chips
sugar strands

TIP

Always popular at school fairs, these cookies look a lot harder to make than they are!

Put the flour in a mixing bowl and blend in the butter using your fingertips until the mixture resembles fine bread crumbs. Stir in the sugar and strawberry jam and mix together with your hands to form a soft ball. Wrap the dough in cling film and chill in the refrigerator for 30 minutes.

Preheat oven to 180°C (gas mark 4). Grease several baking trays or line with nonstick baking parchment.

Roll out the dough to about 5mm thick. Using a 9cm cutter, stamp out stars and lift onto the baking trays. Gather up the remaining dough, roll it out again and cut out more shapes. Bake the cookies for 15 minutes or until lightly golden at the edges. Transfer to a wire rack to cool.

To decorate, melt the chocolate, and use a butter knife to spread to the edges of one side of each cookie. Let the chocolate set a little, but press some sugar strands into the chocolate side before it is completely set. Transfer to a wire rack to cool completely, and store in an airtight container for up to 3 days.

Makes 12

Stars and Moons

These delicious cookies are really buttery, with a crisp coconut texture.

Preparation time: 40 minutes + 30 minutes chilling
Cooking time: 15–20 minutes

115g butter, softened
90g caster sugar
170g plain flour, sifted
40g sweetened dessicated coconut
2 tbsp milk

Decoration
6 tbsp icing sugar, sifted
about 4 tsp water
edible gold dust (optional)

TIP

If you do not chill the dough, it will be sticky and difficult to roll out without adding extra flour. This in turn could make your cookies brittle.

Preheat oven to 180°C (gas mark 4). Grease two baking trays or line with nonstick baking parchment.

In a mixing bowl, beat together the butter and sugar until pale and fluffy. Add the flour to the mixture then add the coconut and milk; mix well. Using your hands, bring the dough together to form a soft ball. Chill in the refrigerator for 30 minutes to firm.

Turn the dough out onto a lightly floured work surface and roll out to 5mm thick. Using a large star cutter, cut out shapes. To make the moon shape, cut out rounds with an 9cm round cutter, then cut away one quarter of the round with the cutter to leave a crescent shape. Gather up the leftover dough, roll it out again and cut out more shapes. Lift the cookies onto the baking trays. Bake for 15–20 minutes or until lightly golden and crisp, then transfer to a wire rack to cool.

To decorate the cookies, mix the icing sugar with sufficient water to form a thin icing. Fill a piping bag with the icing and pipe it carefully onto the cookies to make patterns. Add extra decorations, if desired.

Makes 20

Apple Cookies

Using apple sauce in these cookies creates a smooth texture as well as sweetness.

Preparation time: 35 minutes + 30 minutes chilling
Cooking time: 15–20 minutes

225g plain flour, sifted
90g icing sugar
145g butter, cut into small pieces
3 tbsp apple sauce

Decoration
7 tbsp icing sugar
3 tsp of cold water
green food colouring

TIP

Spice these up a bit by adding 1 tsp of mixed spice to the dough.

Put the flour and icing sugar in a mixing bowl and blend in the butter using your fingertips until the mixture resembles fine bread crumbs. Add the apple sauce and bring the mixture together in a soft ball. Wrap in a sandwich bag and chill in the refrigerator for 30 minutes.

Preheat oven to 180°C (gas mark 4). Grease several baking trays or line with nonstick baking parchment.

On a lightly floured surface, roll out the dough to about 5mm thick. Using a 9cm cutter, stamp out rounds and lift onto the baking trays. Roll out the remaining dough again and cut out more shapes.

Bake the cookies for about 15–20 minutes or until lightly golden at the edges. Transfer to a wire rack.

To decorate, mix the icing sugar with cold water to form a thin icing, adding a few drops of colouring, if desired.

Makes 10

Butterflies

These cookies are made by mixing melted chocolate through the dough, creating a marbled effect.

Preparation time: 25 minutes + 30 minutes chilling
Cooking time: 15 minutes

85g milk chocolate, broken into pieces
115g butter, softened
90g caster sugar
1 egg, beaten
170g plain flour, sifted
icing sugar, for dusting

TIP

If kids are helping to make these, make sure that there is adult supervision when melting the chocolate and using the oven.

Bring a saucepan of water to the boil. When simmering, put the chocolate in a heatproof bowl on top of the saucepan and gently melt the chocolate, stirring until smooth. Remove from the heat and let cool.

In a mixing bowl, beat together the butter and sugar until light and fluffy. Beat in the egg. Stir in the flour and combine all the ingredients to form a soft ball. Add the chocolate and gently stir through to give a marbled effect. Wrap the dough in cling film and chill in the refrigerator for 30 minutes.

Preheat oven to 180°C (gas mark 4). Grease several baking trays or line with nonstick baking parchment.

On a lightly floured surface, roll out the dough to about 5mm thick. Using an 8cm butterfly cutter, stamp out shapes and lift onto the baking trays. Roll out the remaining dough again and cut out more shapes.

Bake the cookies for 15 minutes or until evenly golden brown. Transfer to a wire rack to cool. Just before eating, dust with icing sugar.

Makes 20

Wiggly Animals

This orange shortbread is delicious, so bake double the quantity!

Preparation time: 30 minutes + 30 minutes chilling
Cooking time: 15 minutes

145g butter, softened
90g icing sugar
225g plain flour, sifted
zest of 1 orange
1 tbsp milk

Decoration
155g icing sugar, sifted
4 tsp water

TIP

Wriggly bunnies, teddy bears and even dinosaurs make fun biscuit shapes. Use whatever you can find!

Preheat oven to 180°C (gas mark 4). Grease several baking trays or line with nonstick baking parchment.

In a mixing bowl, beat together the butter and icing sugar until pale and fluffy. Stir in the flour, then add the orange zest and milk. Mix everything together to form a soft dough using your hands. Wrap the dough in cling film and chill in the refrigerator for 30 minutes until firm.

On a lightly floured work surface, roll out the dough to 5mm thick. Using your cutter, cut out your shapes and lift the cookies onto the baking trays. Gather up the leftover dough, roll it out again and cut out more shapes. Bake the cookies for 15 minutes or until lightly golden. Lift them onto a wire rack to cool.

To decorate the animals, mix the icing sugar with sufficient cold water to make a thin icing. Fill a piping bag with the icing and pipe it in a wiggly pattern onto the body of the animals, or use it to mark eyes, ears and noses.

Makes 18

Ice-Cream Cone Cookies

Decorate these cookies with your favourite coloured icing to look like real ice-cream cones with different toppings!

TIP

Serve these at kids' parties together with ice cream.

Preparation time: 40 minutes + 30 minutes chilling
Cooking time: 15 minutes

170g plain flour, sifted
115g butter, cut into small pieces
90g caster sugar
50g dried apricots, chopped
zest of ½ orange
2 tbsp orange juice

Decoration
7 tbsp icing sugar
3 tsp water
food colourings

Preheat oven to 180°C (gas mark 4). Grease several baking trays or line with nonstick baking parchment.

Put the flour in a mixing bowl and blend in the butter using your fingers until the mixture resembles fine bread crumbs. Stir in the sugar, apricots, orange zest and orange juice and mix everything together, using your hands to bring the mixture together in a soft ball. Wrap the dough in cling film and chill in the refrigerator for 30 minutes until firm.

On a lightly floured surface, roll out the dough to about 5mm thick. Using an 11cm heart cutter, stamp out hearts, gather up the leftover dough, roll it out again and cut out more hearts. Cut each heart in half lengthways to create cone shapes and lift onto the baking trays. Using the back of a knife, mark a line across, near the top of the cookie, to mark the top of the cone, then cover the cone area with criss-cross lines. Bake the cookies for 15 minutes or until golden brown. Lift onto a wire rack to cool.

To decorate the cookies, mix the icing sugar with about 3 tsp of cold water to form a thin icing, then add a few drops of your chosen colouring. Using a piping bag, pipe the icing onto the cookies. Let set.

Makes 18

Jewelled Cookie Bars

This a really easy recipe for children to use when they start cooking by themselves as these cookies do not require baking.

Preparation time: 25 minutes + 4 hours to set (up to 24 hours)

280g milk or plain chocolate
255g digestive biscuits
110g multicoloured glacé cherries, chopped
75g raisins

60g dried apricots, chopped
½ cup white chocolate chips
60g flaked almonds

TIP

Children may be safer melting chocolate in the microwave. Break the chocolate into pieces and put in a microwave-proof bowl. Heat on low for 1 minute, stir. Continue to heat in 30-second busts followed by stirring until melted, about 3 minutes.

First, line a 23 x 23cm shallow tin with nonstick baking parchment.

Under adult supervision, melt the chocolate over a pan of simmering water. Break the chocolate into pieces and put in a heatproof bowl and sit on top of the saucepan. Gently melt the chocolate, stirring until smooth.

Using your fingers break up the digestive biscuits into tiny pieces and put in a large mixing bowl. Keeping some of the remaining ingredients for the top of the cookies. Add the remaining ingredients to the crushed cookies. Add the melted chocolate and mix well.

Press the mixture into the tin, level the surface and sprinkle on the remaining ingredients, pressing down gently to set. Leave the tin in the refrigerator for 4 hours or overnight until it sets hard.
Turn out of the tin onto a chopping board and slice into 16 portions.

Makes 16 bars

Peppermint Rings

These cookies are for anyone who loves mint – they have peppermint essence in the dough and a mint-flavoured boiled sweet in the centre.

Preparation time: 30 minutes + 30 minutes chilling
Cooking time: 15 minutes

170g plain flour, sifted
55g icing sugar
115g lightly salted butter, cut into small pieces
1 tsp peppermint essence
1 tbsp water
20 sparkling clear mint sweets

Put the flour and icing sugar in a large mixing bowl and blend in the butter until the mixture resembles fine bread crumbs. Add the peppermint essence and water, then use your hands to bring the mixture together to form a dough. Wrap the dough in cling film and chill in the refrigerator for 30 minutes until firm.

Line several baking trays with nonstick baking parchment.

On a lightly floured work surface, roll out the dough to about 5mm thick. Using a 6cm round cutter, stamp out the middle of each cookie. Unwrap the sweets and put in the gaps. Re-roll the trimmings and cut out more shapes. Chill the cookies in the refrigerator for 15 minutes.

Preheat oven to 180°C (gas mark 4). Bake the cookies for 15 minutes or until lightly golden. Let cool on the baking trays and allow the sweets to harden before lifting onto a wire rack to cool. Store in an airtight container.

Makes 20

Flower Cookies

The children will love these cookies as they contain little pieces of Smarties in the cooked dough.

Preparation time: 40 minutes
Cooking time: 15 minutes

170g plain flour, sifted
115g butter, cut into small pieces
90g caster sugar
3 tbsp Smarties, broken into small
   pieces
2 tbsp milk

Decoration
7 tbsp icing sugar
3 tsp water
yellow and pink food colourings

TIP

Use this as a colour-learning play idea with very young children, getting them to decorate cookies with, say, red and yellow icing on one cookie and blue and green on another.

Preheat oven to 180°C (gas mark 4). Grease several baking trays or line with nonstick baking parchment.

Put the flour in a mixing bowl and blend in the butter using your fingers until the mixture resembles fine bread crumbs. Stir in the sugar, Smarties and milk, bringing the mixture together in a soft ball using your hands.

On a lightly floured surface, roll out the dough to about 5mm thick. Using a 6cm fluted cutter, cut out your shapes and lift the cookies onto the baking trays. Gather up the leftover dough, roll it out again and cut more shapes. Bake the cookies for 15 minutes, then lift them onto a wire rack to cool.

To decorate the flowers, combine the icing sugar and water and mix to a thin icing. Transfer half the icing to another bowl; add a few drops of yellow colouring to one bowl and pink colouring to the other.

Using piping bags, carefully pipe flower patterns in the contrasting colours onto the cookies. Let set.

Makes 20

Mouse Cookies

These cheeky little 'mice' are too cute not to make! If you like, you can dust these cookies with extra cinnamon and icing sugar after they have come out of the oven.

Preparation time: 30 minutes
Cooking time: 20 minutes

170g plain flour, sifted
1 tsp ground cinnamon
115g butter, cut into small pieces
90g caster sugar
2 tbsp milk

Decoration
14 currants, halved
ground cinnamon, for dusting
icing sugar, for dusting

TIP

You could use black licorice laces for the tails instead of dough. Insert a wooden cocktail stick about 1cm into the rear of the mice as soon as they come out of the oven. Remove the cocktail stick, then insert an 8cm piece of licorice. It should adhere to the cookie as it cools.

Preheat oven to 180°C (gas mark 4). Grease several baking trays or line with nonstick baking parchment.

Put the flour and cinnamon in a bowl, then blend in the butter using your fingertips to form fine bread crumbs. Add the sugar and milk and, using your hands, bring the mixture together to form a soft dough.

Divide the dough into 16 equal-sized pieces. Roll 14 pieces into balls using the palms of your hands, then pinch in one side slightly to look like the 'nose' of a mouse.

Divide the remaining 2 balls into 14 little balls and roll each one to a long sausage shape for the tails. Using a little water, attach a tail to the back of each mouse. Position the currants to look like eyes, then using a pair of small scissors, snip into the dough to create ears. Lift the mice onto the baking trays.

Bake the cookies for 20 minutes. Lift onto a wire rack to cool. Serve dusted with cinnamon and icing sugar, if desired.

Makes 14

Children's Names Cookies

Using a banana-flavoured pudding mix in these cookies gives them a real banana boost. Try using other flavours if you prefer.

Preparation time: 40 minutes + 30 minutes chilling
Cooking time: 15 minutes

6 tbsp soft margarine
70g packed caster sugar
1 egg, beaten
170g self-raising flour, sifted
¼ cup banana-flavoured pudding mix

Decoration
55g plus 1 tbsp icing sugar, sifted
2 tbsp water
pink and blue food colouring

In a mixing bowl, beat together the margarine and sugar until pale and fluffy. Beat in the egg, then add the flour and banana pudding mix. Knead the mixture together with your hands until it comes together in a soft ball. Chill the dough in cling film in the refrigerator for 30 minutes.

Preheat oven to 180°C (gas mark 4). Grease two baking trays or line with nonstick baking parchment.

Sprinkle some flour on the work surface and a rolling pin. Roll out the dough to about 5mm thick. Using a 6cm square cutter, cut out your cookies and lift onto the baking trays. Gather up the leftover dough, roll it out again and cut out more shapes. Bake for 15 minutes or until lightly golden, then transfer to a wire rack to cool.

To decorate the squares, mix the icing sugar with sufficient water to form a thin icing. Keeping about 3 tablespoons of the icing in the bowl, put the remaining icing in two bowls and colour one pink and one blue. Fill piping bags with the icings. Pipe boys' names with the blue icing on half the cookies and girls' names with the pink icing on the remainder. The white icing can then be used to make a border if there is space. Eat on the day the cookies are iced.

Makes 15

Gingerbread Family

These crunchy ginger cookies are fun to make, and glazing them with egg white and sugar makes all the difference.

**Preparation time: 30 minutes +
  2 hours chilling**
Cooking time: 8–12 minutes

350g plain flour
¾ tsp bicarbonate of soda
2 tsp ground ginger
1 tsp ground cinnamon
¼ tsp ground nutmeg
¼ tsp ground cloves

115g unsalted butter, room
  temperature
90g white sugar
1 large egg
⅔ cup treacle

Decoration
115g icing sugar
1–2 tbsp water
edible black pen

TIP

These cookies can be used as fun, edible gift tags: simply punch a hole with a drinking straw, and thread ribbon through.

Sift the flour, bicarbonate of soda and spices into a large bowl and set aside.

In a medium saucepan, melt together the butter, sugar and treacle. Let cool, and then whisk in the egg. Add the flour mixture and combine. Set in a cool place for at least 2 hours, until dough is firm.

Preheat oven to 190°C (gas mark 5). Grease two baking trays or line with nonstick baking parchment. Roll out dough to 5mm thick, and use people-shaped cutters to cut out shapes. Place on baking sheets, and bake for 8–12 minutes depending on size of cookies. Transfer cookies to a wire rack to cool.

To decorate, slowly add water to the icing sugar, until mixture is loose enough to pipe, but not watery. Spoon into a piping bag fitted with a small nozzle, and pipe faces, buttons and skirts onto the cookies. When set, fill in details with edible pen.

Makes about 36, depending on size of cutters

Gingerbread Selection

These cookies are just as good as traditional gingerbread but with currants in the mixture. You can use any biscuit cutter you like.

Preparation time: 40 minutes + 30 minutes chilling
Cooking time: 8–10 minutes

55g packed soft brown sugar
3 tbsp golden syrup
½ tsp ground cinnamon
½ tsp ground ginger
1½ tbsp butter
225g plain flour, sifted
1 tsp baking powder

1 egg, beaten
75g currants, chopped

Decoration
40g icing sugar, sifted
4 tsp water
green food colouring

TIP

If you really love the flavour of ginger, omit the currants & replace with finely chopped candied ginger.

Grease two baking trays or line with nonstick baking parchment. Dissolve the sugar, syrup, spices and butter together in a saucepan. Stir over low heat until they have melted.

Sift the flour and baking powder into a mixing bowl, then add the syrup mixture, beaten egg and the currants. Mix everything together, then knead the mixture into a ball using your hands. Chill the dough in cling film in the refrigerator for 30 minutes.

Preheat oven to 170°C (gas mark 3). Sprinkle some flour on the work surface and a rolling pin. Roll out the dough thinly to about 5mm thick. Using the cutters, cut out your shapes and lift the cookies onto baking trays. Gather up the leftover dough, roll it out again and cut out more shapes. Bake the cookies for 8–10 minutes or until they are golden brown, then lift them onto a wire rack to cool.

To complete the gingerbread selection, mix the icing sugar with sufficient water to make a thin icing and add a few drops of green colouring. Using a piping bag, pipe onto the cookies and decorate.

Makes 24

Red Heart Cookies

Who can resist a crisp cookie base filled with lots of strawberry jam?
Use a different flavoured jam if you prefer.

Preparation time: 30 minutes + 30 minutes chilling
Cooking time: 20 minutes

170g plain flour, sifted
25g ground almonds
115g butter, softened
50g caster sugar

2 tbsp milk
1 egg, beaten
4 tbsp strawberry jam

TIP

Remember to check
that none of the kids
you are entertaining
has a nut allergy when
making this cookie.

Put the flour and ground almonds in a mixing bowl, then blend in the butter
until the mixture resembles fine bread crumbs. Stir in the sugar and milk and,
using your hands, work the mixture together to form a dough. Wrap in cling
film and chill in the refrigerator for 30 minutes.

Preheat oven to 180°C (gas mark 4). Grease two baking trays or line with
nonstick baking parchment.

On a lightly floured surface, roll out the dough and cut out 12 8cm hearts with
a cutter. Put these onto the baking trays and prick with a fork. Cut out 12
more heart shapes with the 8cm cutter, then remove the centre of these
using a 5cm heart cutter to leave a heart outline.

Using a pastry brush, apply the beaten egg to the large heart cookies.
Top with a heart 'outline' and seal around the edges. Brush the
whole cookie with more beaten egg. Bake the cookies
for 20 minutes or until golden. Lift onto a wire rack
to cool.

Once the cookies have cooled, spoon the jam onto
each, keeping within the heart shape in the centre.

Makes 12

Clock Cookies

These cookies are flavoured with sultanas and cut into circles to make big clock faces. Pipe the icing to make different times on each cookie!

Preparation time: 35 minutes + 30 minutes chilling
Cooking time: 15–20 minutes

85g soft margarine
140g caster sugar
1 egg, beaten
170g plain flour, sifted
80g sultanas

Decoration
115g icing sugar
1 tbsp cold water

In a mixing bowl, beat together the margarine and sugar until light and fluffy. Beat in the egg. Stir in the flour and sultanas and, using your hands, bring all the mixture together in a soft ball. Wrap the dough in cling film and chill in the refrigerator for 30 minutes.

Preheat oven to 180°C (gas mark 4). Grease several baking trays or line with nonstick baking parchment.

On a lightly floured surface, roll out the dough to about 5mm thick. Using a 10cm round cutter, stamp out rounds and lift onto the baking trays. Gather up the remaining dough, roll it again and cut out more shapes. Bake the cookies for 15–20 minutes or until evenly golden. Transfer to a wire rack to cool.

To decorate the 'clocks', mix the icing sugar with about 1 tablespoon of cold water to form a thin icing. Using a piping bag, pipe the numbers 12, 3, 6 and 9 onto the circles in the correct clock positions. Then pipe an 'hour' hand and 'minute' hand to make different 'times' on each cookie. Let set.

Makes 10

Fruit Segments

These look just like a segment of fruit and they are full of citrus flavours.

Preparation time: 25 minutes + 30 minutes chilling
Cooking time: 15 minutes

115g butter, softened
70g caster sugar
1 egg, separated
200g plain flour, sifted

zest of 1 lemon
zest of 1 orange
2 tbsp orange juice
granulated sugar, for sprinkling

Preheat oven to 180°C (gas mark 4). Grease two baking trays or line with nonstick baking parchment.

In a mixing bowl, beat together the butter and sugar until pale and fluffy, then beat in the egg yolk. Stir in the flour, zests and orange juice and mix everything together. Using your hands, bring the dough together to form a ball. Wrap in cling film and refrigerate for 30 minutes.

Turn the dough out onto a lightly floured work surface and roll out to 5mm thick. Using 9cm round cutter, cut out rounds then cut each circle in half to make the segments. Gather up the leftover dough, roll it out again and cut out more shapes.

In a small bowl, whisk the egg white slightly with a fork and, using a pastry brush, glaze each cookie and sprinkle with a little extra sugar. Bake the cookies for 15 minutes or until lightly golden and crisp. Lift them onto a wire rack to cool. When cold, store them in an airtight container.

Makes 16

> ## TIP
>
> Try topping these with cinnamon orange sugar: Combine 90g sugar with 1 tablespoon cinnamon and the zest of 1 orange. Then store in an airtight container for at least a week to mature before using.

Cookies for Special Diets

Some people believe that being on a special diet puts an end to treats such as cookies; this is definitely not the case. You can still enjoy sweet temptations – you simply have to use a little more ingenuity.

Cookies for Special Diets

This chapter is full of recipes specially created for those with specific dietary requirements. These cookies are not naughty at all, but are nevertheless so nice that they will become firm favourites with the whole family.

Cookies can play their part in a high-fibre diet too – with tasty treats such as the Caribbean Lime Cookies, the Sesame Oat Crisps and the Peanut and Raisin Cookies. The Wheat-Free Fruity Oat Bars also provide an excellent addition to the lunchbox or an on-the-run breakfast, while the Simple Macaroons are a guilt-free treat that can be enjoyed by nearly everyone.

Many of the recipes retain butter as a principle ingredient because butter really does give cookies that magical richness of flavour. Reduced-fat margarines and spreads cannot always be substituted for butter because their high water content prevents cookies from crisping up satisfactorily. Take heart, though – a solution comes in the form of the Apple and Raisin Cookies, which exploit an inventive technique of using apple sauce to reduce the need for fat. For the same reason, you'll be astonished by the virtuous, prune-based Brownies, which manage to be amazingly delicious and yet almost fat free.

Coconut Crisps

These high-fibre cookies are deliciously light and crispy and simply melt in the mouth. They are very quick and easy to make too.

Preparation time: 10 minutes
Cooking time: 15 minutes

115g lightly salted butter	50g sweetened dessicated coconut
1 generous tbsp golden syrup	115g plain flour
90g raw sugar	1 tsp bicarbonate of soda
90g rolled oats	1 tsp hot water

Preheat oven to 180˚C (gas mark 4). Grease or line two baking trays with nonstick baking parchment.

Put the butter, syrup and sugar in a large saucepan. Heat the mixture gently until the butter has melted and the sugar has dissolved. Stir in the rolled oats and flour and mix well. Dissolve the bicarbonate of soda in the hot water and stir into the mixture. Let cool slightly.

Roll heaped teaspoonfuls of the mixture into walnut-sized balls, then put onto the baking trays, allowing plenty of space for the mixture to spread. Bake for 15 minutes or until evenly browned. Let cool slightly, then use a thin metal spatula to transfer to a wire rack to cool completely. Store for up to one week in an airtight container.

Makes about 20

TIP

Dissolving bicarbonate of soda in hot water makes it react more quickly, creating loads of vigorous bubbles to lighten the batter. This results in a nicely crisp cookie.

Peanut and Raisin Cookies

Diets that contain a daily intake of peanuts, peanut butter or peanut oil may help protect against heart disease.

Preparation time: 15 minutes
Cooking time: 15–20 minutes

115g lightly salted butter,
  melted
140g caster sugar
1 egg, beaten
5 tsp baking powder

225g crunchy peanut butter
90g plain flour
90g wholemeal flour
150g raisins

TIP

Ring the changes by using a mix of hazelnuts and apricots or pecans and dried cranberries.

Preheat oven to 190°C (gas mark 5). Grease or line two baking trays with nonstick baking parchment.

Put all the ingredients except the raisins into a bowl and beat together until well blended. Stir in the raisins. Spoon heaped teaspoonfuls of the mixture onto the baking trays, spaced well apart to allow the mixture to spread. Bake for 15–20 minutes or until brown around the edges.

Let cool slightly then, using a thin metal spatula, transfer to a wire rack to cool completely. Store for up to one week in an airtight container.

Makes about 20

Low-Fat Banana and Carob Cookies

Bananas are an excellent source of potassium and rich in vitamin B6. If you can't get hold of carob chips, substitute chocolate chips, but they will increase the fat content.

TIP

Sift the baking powder in with the plain flour to avoid lumps.

Preparation time: 15 minutes
Cooking time: 15–20 minutes

2 medium bananas, mashed
70g caster sugar
2 eggs, beaten
90g plain flour, sifted
55g plain wholemeal flour
1 tsp baking powder
½ cup roughly chopped banana chips
130g roughly chopped dates

Preheat oven to 190°C (gas mark 5). Grease or line two baking trays with nonstick baking parchment.

Beat together the banana and sugar until well combined. In a separate bowl, beat the eggs until fluffy, and then add to the banana and sugar mixture. Stir in both flours, baking powder, banana chips and dates.

With floured hands, roll the dough into balls the size of walnuts. Put onto the baking trays, spaced well apart to let the mixture spread. Bake for 15–20 minutes or until brown around the edges. Let cool slightly, then use a thin metal spatula to transfer to a wire rack to cool completely. Store for up to one week in an airtight container.

Makes about 15

Caribbean Lime Cookies

Dried tropical fruits are readily available and make a good alternative to dried apricots.

Preparation time: 15 minutes
Cooking time: 15–20 minutes

115g lightly salted butter
150g caster sugar
1 egg, beaten
90g plain flour
1 level tsp baking powder

55g wholemeal flour
130g chopped dried mango
50g sweetened dessicated
   coconut
zest of 2 limes

Preheat oven to 190°C (gas mark 5). Grease or line two baking trays with nonstick baking parchment.

Beat together the butter and sugar until soft. Beat in the egg. Sift the plain flour and the baking powder. Stir in both flours, mango, coconut and lime zest.

With floured hands roll the dough into walnut-sized balls. Put onto the baking trays, allowing enough space for the mixture to spread. Bake in the oven for 15–20 minutes or until brown around the edges. Let cool slightly, then use a thin metal spatula to transfer to a wire rack to cool completely. Store for up to one week in an airtight container.

Makes about 15

TIP

If your cookies always brown too much on the bottom, check that you are not using a dark-coloured baking tray, which will absorb more heat than a paler one. Try using a heavy gauge metal tray instead.

Apricot and Almond Cookies

Dried apricots provide good amounts of betacarotene, potassium and soluble fibre. They are also a useful source of iron.

Preparation time: 15 minutes
Cooking time: 15–20 minutes

115g lightly salted butter
70g caster sugar
1 egg, beaten
90g plain flour
1 tsp baking powder

90g wholemeal flour
115g roughly chopped dried
 apricots
90g flaked almonds
1 tsp almond essence

TIP

Using half plain flour and half wholemeal flour increases the fibre in the cookies without compromising their lightness.

Preheat oven to 190°C (gas mark 5). Grease or line two baking trays with nonstick baking parchment.

Beat together the butter and sugar until soft. Beat in the egg. Sift the plain flour together with the baking powder. Stir in both types of flour, as well as the apricots, almonds and almond essence.

With floured hands roll the dough into walnut-sized balls. Put onto the baking trays, allowing enough space for the mixture to spread. Bake for 15–20 minutes or until brown around the edges. Let cool slightly, then transfer to a wire rack to cool completely. Store for up to one week in an airtight container.

Makes 15–20

Sesame Oat Crisps

Sesame seeds are a good source of calcium and vitamin E and add a delicious nutty flavour to these cookies.

Preparation time: 10 minutes
Cooking time: 15 minutes

115g lightly salted butter
1¼ tbsp golden syrup
90g raw sugar
70g rolled oats

⅓ cup sesame seeds
115g plain flour
1 tsp bicarbonate of soda
1 tsp hot water

TIP

If you take two of these cookies for lunch, wrap the cookies in pairs back to back to reduce the risk of breakage.

Preheat oven to 180°C (gas mark 4). Grease or line two baking trays with nonstick baking parchment.

Put the butter, syrup and sugar in a large saucepan. Heat the mixture gently until the butter has melted and the sugar dissolved. Stir in rolled oats, sesame seeds and flour and mix well. Dissolve the bicarbonate of soda in the hot water and stir into the mixture. Let cool slightly.

Roll heaped teaspoonfuls of the mixture into walnut-sized balls. Put onto the baking trays, allowing plenty of space for the mixture to spread as it bakes. Bake for 15 minutes or until evenly browned. Remove from the oven and cool slightly, then use a thin metal spatula to transfer them to a wire rack to cool completely. Store for up to one week in an airtight container.

Makes about 20

Ginger Thins

These cookies contain around a third of a teaspoon of fat each. Serve them with frozen yoghurt or reduced-fat ice cream.

Preparation time: 10 minutes
Cooking time: 7 minutes

1 tbsp unsalted butter
1 tbsp icing sugar
3 tbsp golden syrup

2 tbsp plain flour
1 level tsp ground ginger
pinch of salt

> **TIP**
> Ground ginger looses its potency quickly, so store it in a cool, dark place and replace it as soon as it is out of date.

Preheat oven to 190°C (gas mark 5). Grease or line two baking trays with nonstick baking parchment.

Put the butter, icing sugar and syrup in a small saucepan and gently heat until the sugar has dissolved. Remove from the heat and cool slightly.

Sift together the flour, ginger and salt and stir into the butter mixture.

Put small spoonfuls of the mixture onto the prepared baking trays, allowing plenty of space for the mixture to spread. Bake for 7 minutes or until golden brown. Let the cookies to cool on the tray for about 30 seconds. Using a thin metal spatula, carefully lift the cookies off the baking tray and while they are still warm and pliable, shape them over an oiled rolling pin or tall glass. Once set, transfer to a wire rack to cool completely. The thins can also be left in their original flat shapes, if preferred. Store for up to one week in an airtight container.

Makes about 10

Treacle Cookies

These cookies contain just under half a teaspoon of fat. Oatmeal is rich in soluble fibre, which can help reduce high blood cholesterol levels.

Preparation time: 10 minutes
Cooking time: 20 minutes

115g self-raising flour
55g fine oatmeal
3 tbsp caster sugar

¼ cup treacle
30g lightly salted butter
2 tbsp skimmed milk

TIP

You could also make these cookies quite successfully with thick honey instead of treacle.

Preheat oven to 190°C (gas mark 5). Grease or line two baking trays with nonstick baking parchment.

Mix all the dry ingredients in a bowl. Put the treacle and butter in a small saucepan and gently heat until the butter has melted. Pour the treacle mixture onto the dry ingredients, add the milk and mix to make smooth dough.

Knead the dough on a lightly floured surface, then roll out to almost 1cm thick. Cut out small rectangular cookies from the dough, or use a 5cm round cutter to cut out circles, then transfer your shapes to the baking trays. Using a sharp knife, make shallow cuts across the surface and bake for 20 minutes or until firm to the touch. Transfer to wire rack to cool. Store for up to one week in an airtight container.

Makes about 15

Lemon and Poppy Seed Cookies

Poppy seeds give these healthy gluten-free cookies an added crunch.

Preparation time: 15 minutes + 30 minutes chilling
Cooking time: 15–20 minutes

115g lightly salted butter or margarine
90g caster sugar
1 egg, beaten
170g gluten-free flour
zest of 2 lemons
2 tbsp poppy seeds

TIP

Gluten-free flours are free from wheat; however wheat gluten makes dough strong and elastic and helps mixtures rise. Therefore, gluten-free flour cannot simply be substituted for wheat flour in all recipes.

Preheat oven to 180°C (gas mark 4). Grease or line two baking trays with nonstick baking parchment.

Beat together the butter and sugar until light and fluffy. Gradually beat in the egg. Add in the gluten-free flour, lemon zest and poppy seeds and mix well. Wrap in cling film and chill in the refrigerator for 30 minutes.

On a lightly floured surface, roll the dough out to 5mm thick. Using a 5cm round or fluted cutter, cut out the cookies, then transfer them to the baking trays and bake for 15–20 minutes. Let cool slightly on the baking trays then, using a thin metal spatula, carefully transfer them to a wire rack to cool completely.

Makes about 36

Sour Cherry and Oatmeal Cookies

Oats are an excellent source of soluble fibre, which can help reduce high blood cholesterol levels, thereby lessening the risk of heart disease.

Preparation time: 15 minutes
Cooking time: 15–20 minutes

115g plain flour
½ tsp bicarbonate of soda
½ tsp baking powder
½ tsp salt
115g unsalted butter
115g dark brown sugar
1 egg, beaten

1 tsp vanilla essence
1 tbsp milk
zest of 1 large orange
160g rolled oats
130g sour cherries, roughly
   chopped

TIP

Dark brown sugar gives a rich caramel flavour to these cookies that you would find lacking if you substituted regular granulated sugar.

Preheat oven to 180°C (gas mark 4). Grease or line two baking trays with nonstick baking parchment.

Sift together the flour, bicarbonate of soda, baking powder and salt. Beat together the butter and sugar. Gradually add the egg, vanilla and milk and beat until smooth. Stir in the sifted ingredients and mix well. Stir in the orange zest, oats and sour cherries.

Place tablespoonfuls of dough spaced well apart on the baking trays to allow the mixture to spread. Bake for 15–20 minutes or until just brown. Remove from the oven and let the cookies cool slightly, then using a thin metal spatula, transfer to a wire rack to cool completely.

Store for up to one week in an airtight container.

Makes 15–20

Low-Fat Chocolate Brownies

These brownies contain a fraction of the fat in traditional brownies.

Preparation time: 15 minutes
Cooking time: 25–30 minutes

225g ready-to-eat prunes
3 tbsp water
115g plain chocolate
3 egg whites
225g light brown sugar

1 tsp salt
1 tsp vanilla essence
55g plain flour, sifted
50g pecans, chopped

TIP

Prune and apple purée are great healthy replacements for fat in baking because they stabilise the batter in much the same way as fat does.

Preheat oven to 180˚C (gas mark 4). Grease and line the base of a 20 x 20cm shallow baking tin with nonstick baking parchment.

Using a blender, blend the prunes with the water until they make a smooth paste. Break the chocolate into a bowl and put over a saucepan of simmering water. Stir occasionally until the chocolate has melted. Remove from the heat and set aside to cool slightly.

In a bowl, mix together the prune purée, melted chocolate, egg whites, sugar, salt and vanilla essence. Fold in the sifted flour.

Pour the mixture into the prepared tin, sprinkle with pecans and bake for about 25–30 minutes or until firm to the touch. Leave in the tin to cool completely. Store, covered in the tin, for up to three days.

Makes 9

Muesli Cookies

Swiss muesli is high in fibre and rich in vitamins.

Preparation time: 10 minutes
Cooking time: 15–20 minutes

115g lightly salted butter or margarine
70g raw sugar
1 egg, beaten
115g sugar-free muesli
55g wholemeal flour
1¼ tsp baking powder

TIP

Avoid using muesli that contains very large chunks of fruit and nuts, or remove these and chop them into smaller pieces.

Preheat oven to 190°C (gas mark 5). Grease or line two baking trays with nonstick baking parchment.

Beat together the butter and sugar until light and fluffy. Gradually beat in the egg. Stir in the muesli, flour and baking powder and mix well. Roll into balls the size of a walnut and put onto the baking trays, allowing space for the cookies to spread. Using the palm of your hand, flatten the cookies slightly.

Bake the cookies for 15–20 minutes. Let cool slightly on the baking trays, then use a thin metal spatula to transfer to a wire rack to cool completely. Store in an airtight container.

Makes about 15

Wheat-Free Fruity Oat Bars

Sunflower seeds are a rich source of vitamin E, the B vitamins thiamin and niacin and the mineral zinc. A great lunchbox cookie.

Preparation time: 30 minutes
Cooking time: 30 minutes

115g unsalted butter or margarine
115g light brown sugar
1 tbsp golden syrup
160g rolled oats
50g sultanas

50g roughly chopped dried
  apricots
1 tsp mixed spice
50g plus 1 tbsp sunflower
  seeds

> **TIP**
>
> Try using blueberry fruit syrup instead of the golden syrup and replacing the sultanas with dried blueberries.

Preheat oven to 180°C (gas mark 4). Lightly grease and base-line a shallow 20 x 20cm baking tin.

Heat the butter, sugar and syrup in a saucepan until dissolved. Remove from the heat, add the remaining ingredients and mix well. Spoon the mixture into the prepared tin, level the surface and bake in the oven for about 30 minutes or until golden brown.

Leave to cool for 5 minutes in the tin, then cut into 9 pieces. When cold, transfer to an airtight container. Don't try to remove the bars from the tin while they are still warm because they will break.

Makes 9

Simple Macaroons

These classic cookies use no flour whatsoever, so are both gluten- and wheat-free. They are low in saturated fat too.

Preparation time: 10 minutes
Cooking time: 25 minutes

1 egg white
115g icing sugar, sifted
170g ground almonds
115g flaked almonds

TIP

Traditionally, macaroons are cooked on edible rice paper. You can use this instead of parchment, if you like.

Preheat oven to 150°C (gas mark 2). Line two baking trays with nonstick baking parchment.

Whisk the egg whites in a bowl until stiff but not dry. Gently fold in the icing sugar and ground almonds until the mixture becomes a sticky dough.

Spoon walnut-sized balls of mixture onto the baking trays, leaving plenty of space in between. Distribute the flaked almonds evenly across the tops of each macaroon. Bake for about 25 minutes; the outer crust should be golden and the inside soft. Transfer to a wire rack to cool. Store for up to one week in an airtight container.

Makes about 24

Apple and Raisin Cookies

Apple sauce has been used to replace some of the fat in these cookies.

Preparation time: 15 minutes
Cooking time: 15–20 minutes

60g lightly salted butter or margarine
90g caster sugar
½ cup unsweetened apple sauce
1 egg yolk
150g plain flour

60g rolled oats
½ tsp bicarbonate of soda
½ tsp baking powder
50g raisins
40g chopped walnuts

TIP

Prune and Raisin Cookies Simply substitute puréed prunes for the apple sauce.

Preheat oven to 190°C (gas mark 5). Line two baking trays with nonstick baking parchment.

Beat together the butter and sugar until light and fluffy. Beat in the apple sauce and egg yolk. Add the flour, oats, bicarbonate of soda, baking powder, raisins and walnuts and beat to make a soft dough.

With lightly floured hands, roll the mixture into walnut-sized balls and put onto the baking trays, allowing space for the cookies to spread. Using the palm of your hand, flatten the cookies slightly and bake for 15–20 minutes until set. Let cool slightly on the baking tray, then transfer to a wire rack to cool. Store for up to one week in an airtight container.

Makes 15–18

Celebration Cookies

Celebrations are all about joy, laughter and indulgence.
So what could fit the bill better than flamboyant cookies bursting
with rich fruits and nuts and decorated to the hilt in brilliant
colours, sparkling sugar and cute little sweets?

Celebration Cookies

Celebrations and special days call for treats and pampering. They are a time to enjoy the good things that life has to offer and share them with friends and family. It is no wonder that there are cookies associated with festivals and feast days throughout the world. The very best ingredients that a country has to offer are brought together for these occasions, resulting in the most wonderful and indulgent cookies, full of dried fruit, nuts, chocolate and exotic spices.

This chapter begins with Christmas and has a range of international favourites catering to the tastes of both young and old. There are bright and playful Cinnamon Candy Trees and Stained-Glass Windows; then the more traditional Spiced Christmas Cookies and the delicious Kourambiedes, without which no Greek Christmas would be complete.

Thanksgiving wouldn't be Thanksgiving without the appearance of pumpkins and here we have some Pumpkin Fingers to celebrate the day. Then there are a few cookies for Passover and Hanukkah, some for Easter and St Patrick's Day, and some, of course, for the Feast of St Valentine.

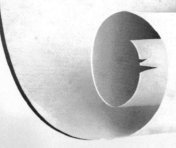

Cinnamon Sweet Trees

These crisp cinnamon Christmas cookies are decorated with tangy jelly sweets.

Preparation time: 30 minutes + 30 minutes chilling
Cooking time: 15 minutes

115g unsalted butter	**Icing**
50g caster sugar	25g icing sugar
150g plain flour	1 tsp. lemon juice
½ tsp. ground cinnamon	90g small jelly sweets
40g rice flour	

Preheat oven to 180°C (gas mark 4). Line two large baking trays with nonstick baking parchment.

Beat the butter in a bowl until soft, then gradually mix in the sugar. Stir in the flour, cinnamon and rice flour until well mixed, then knead lightly. Roll out on a lightly floured surface to 5mm thick. Wrap in cling film and chill for at least 30 minutes.

Cut out 20 8cm tree shapes. Lift onto the baking trays, spacing slightly apart. Bake for 15 minutes, until lightly golden. Leave on the baking trays for a few minutes, then remove and cool on wire racks. Sift the icing sugar into a small bowl and stir in the lemon juice to make a smooth icing. Dip the bases of the jelly sweets into the icing and stick onto the trees. Leave to set.

Makes 20

> **TIP**
> Make chocolate sweet trees by substituting 25g unsweetened cocoa powder for the same amount of flour, and then continue with the recipe.

Spiced Winter Cookies

With their crunchy, sugary topping and warm spicy flavouring, these cookies taste equally good served with steaming hot punch or for afternoon tea.

Preparation time: 30 minutes + 1 hour chilling
Cooking time: 10–12 minutes

115g unsalted butter, softened
75g light brown sugar
1 egg, separated
150g plain flour, sifted
1 tsp. ground cinnamon
½ tsp. ground ginger
¼ tsp. freshly grated nutmeg
¼ tsp. ground cloves
cinnamon and icing sugar, to dust.

TIP

If you want to hang these cookies on the Christmas tree, omit the dusting of icing sugar and cinnamon, and brush with egg white and sprinkle with sugar before baking.

Preheat oven to 180°C (gas mark 4). Line two baking trays with nonstick baking parchment.

Beat the butter and sugar together until light and fluffy. Add the egg to the mixture and mix well. Stir in the flour and spices to make a soft dough. Wrap in cling film and leave to chill in the refrigerator for 1 hour.

Roll out the dough about 5mm thick on a lightly floured surface. Cut into Christmas shapes with floured 6cm cutters.

Transfer the cookies to the baking trays. Bake for 10–12 minutes. Leave for 1–2 minutes before lifting off the cookie sheets and cooling on wire racks. Dust with icing sugar and cinnamon to finish.

Makes about 20

Stained-Glass Windows

These cookies look wonderful hanging on the Christmas tree with light shining through.

TIP

Dip your cutters lightly in flour to prevent them sticking to the rich dough.

Preparation time: 45 minutes
Cooking time: 8–10 minutes

225g plain flour
140g lightly salted butter
150g caster sugar
zest of 1 orange
1 egg yolk
boiled sweets, preferably clear with bright colours

Preheat oven to 190°C (gas mark 5). Line two large baking trays with nonstick baking parchment.

Sift the flour into a bowl. Blend in the butter until the mixture resembles bread crumbs. Stir in the sugar and orange zest. Add the egg yolk and mix to a dough.

Knead on a lightly floured surface for a few seconds, then roll out to 2mm thickness. Using Christmas cutters, cut out various festive shapes. Cut out the centres, leaving a border of at least 5mm all round. If you want to hang these from the tree, cut a hole in each to thread a ribbon through later. Transfer to the baking trays.

Put the boiled sweets into plastic bags and coarsely crush with a rolling pin. Sprinkle the crushed sweets in the cut-out centres of the cookies. Bake for 8–10 minutes, until the cookies are golden and the sweets have melted. Leave to cool completely on the baking trays. Eat within 10 days.

Makes about 20

Snowballs

These little coconut cookies are sandwiched together in pairs, then coated in even more coconut to look like snowballs.

Preparation time: 35 minutes
Cooking time: 15–20 minutes

170g lightly salted butter
200g caster sugar
2 egg yolks
350g plain flour
½ tsp. baking soda
75g sweetened dessicated coconut
2 tbsp. milk

Decoration
115g white chocolate
1 cup apricot jam
225g sweetened dessicated coconut

TIP

If your coconut flakes are too large to stick to the cookies, put them in the food processor and pulse them a few times to get a slightly finer shred.

Preheat oven to 190°C (gas mark 5). Lightly grease two baking trays or line with nonstick baking parchment.

Beat the butter and sugar together until light and fluffy. Add the egg yolks and beat well. Sift the flour and baking soda together, work into the butter mixture then add the dessicated coconut and milk. Divide the mixture into 24 pieces and shape into balls. Put onto the baking trays, spacing them 4cm apart to allow for spreading. Bake for 15–20 minutes, or until golden brown. Remove from the baking trays and cool on a wire rack.

Break the white chocolate into squares and put in a small bowl over a pan of near-boiling water. Stir occasionally until melted. Dip one cookie into the chocolate and sandwich together with a second cookie to make 12 pairs. Leave to set for 20 minutes.

Heat the apricot jam in a small pan until melted, then press through a sieve. Brush over the cookies, then roll in the coconut to coat.

Makes 12

Cherry Garlands

These pretty piped cookies are decorated with glacé cherries and angelica.

Preparation time: 40 minutes
Cooking time: 15–20 minutes

55g icing sugar
240g soft margarine
225g plain flour
55g cornflour
½ tsp. almond essence
60g glacé cherries, chopped very fine
glacé cherries and crystallised angelica, to decorate
1 tbsp. icing sugar, to dredge

Preheat oven to 190°C (gas mark 5). Lightly grease two baking trays or line with nonstick baking parchment.

Sift the icing sugar into a bowl. Add the margarine and cream together until light and fluffy. Sift the flour and cornflour together and beat into the mixture with the almond essence and the chopped glacé cherries.

Spoon half the mixture into a piping bag fitted with a 1cm star nozzle. Pipe 5cm rings onto the baking trays, spacing them apart. Decorate each cookie with quartered glacé cherries and pieces of angelica. Bake for 15–20 minutes until pale golden. Leave on the baking trays for a few minutes, then transfer to a wire rack and let cool. Dredge with icing sugar before serving. Store cooled cookies in an airtight container with nonstick paper between the layers.

Makes about 20

> **TIP**
>
> Angelica is from the same plant family as parsley. It is a graceful and aromatic herb that looks great in the garden – and it's simple to crystallise the stems at home.

Rum-Glazed Wreaths

These cookies look impressive, but are very simple to make.

Preparation time: 35 minutes
Cooking time: 15 minutes

85g lightly salted butter
75g light brown sugar
170g plain flour
½ tsp. vanilla essence
1 tbsp. milk

Glaze
115g icing sugar
4 tsp. dark rum, orange liqueur or lemon juice

TIP

Taking care to mould the cookies to a uniform size before baking them is worth the effort. Not only do they look nicer, they cook more evenly too.

Preheat oven to 190°C (gas mark 5). Lightly grease two baking trays or line with nonstick baking parchment.

Beat the butter and sugar until light and fluffy. Sift the flour and work into the mixture along with the vanilla essence and milk. On a floured surface, lightly knead the dough for a few seconds.

Divide the dough into 16 pieces, then divide each piece into 8 and roll into balls. Arrange the balls in rings on the baking trays, touching each other. Bake for 15 minutes until golden. Leave the balls to cool on the baking trays.

For the glaze, sift the icing sugar into a bowl and stir in the rum, orange liqueur or lemon juice. Brush over the cookies and leave to set on a wire rack before serving.

Makes 16

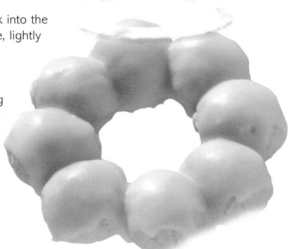

Winter Logs

Dipping these meltingly light chocolate cookies in chocolate makes them twice as nice.

Preparation time: 35 minutes
Cooking time: 12 minutes

170g unsalted butter, softened
40g icing sugar
½ tsp. vanilla essence
150g plain flour
25g unsweetened cocoa powder
40g cornflour
115g plain chocolate
1 tbsp. icing sugar, for dusting

> **TIP**
>
> These look great decorated with a tiny robin. These are often found in craft shops that sell Christmas cake decorations.

Preheat oven to 180°C (gas mark 4). Line two baking trays with nonstick baking parchment.

Beat the butter, sugar and vanilla essence together until light and fluffy. Sift the flour, cocoa powder and cornflour together and fold in.

Spoon the mixture into a piping bag fitted with a 1cm star nozzle. Pipe 6cm lengths onto the baking trays, spacing well apart. Bake the logs for 12 minutes, then remove from the baking trays and transfer to wire racks to cool.

Melt the chocolate in a bowl over a pan of near-boiling water. Dip both ends of the logs into the chocolate and leave to set on nonstick baking parchment. Dust the logs with icing sugar before serving.

Makes about 35

Kourambiedes

These rich, tender almond cookies are served at all festive occasions in Greece. At Christmas they often bury a whole clove in the cookies to symbolise the gifts the three wise men brought to the Christ child.

Preparation time: 25 minutes + 1 hour chilling
Cooking time: 15–20 minutes

60g blanched almonds, lightly toasted and cooled
230g unsalted butter
2 tbsp. icing sugar
¼ tsp. salt
1 small egg yolk
1 tbsp. brandy, orange-flavoured liqueur or orange flower water
225g plain flour
icing sugar, for dusting

TIP

If you're worried about your guests being shocked at biting into a whole clove, bury a jumbo raisin inside the cookies instead to symbolise the gifts of the three wise men.

In a food processor fitted with a metal blade, process the cooled toasted almonds until very fine crumbs are formed.

In a medium bowl, beat the butter until soft, then beat in the sugar until the mixture becomes light and fluffy. Beat in the salt, egg yolk, and brandy or orange flower water until combined. Stir in the flour and ground almonds until a soft dough forms. Refrigerate, covered, until firm for about 1 hour.

Preheat oven to 230°C (gas mark 8).

Use a tablespoon to scoop out dough, and form into 3cm balls. Put on ungreased baking trays, and bake until set and just golden, for about 15–20 minutes. Let cool slightly, then transfer the cookies onto wire racks to cool completely. Dust with icing sugar. Store in an airtight container.

Makes about 30

Cookie Candy Canes

This cane dough can be shaped into candy canes or Christmas wreaths, then tinted whatever colour you like.

Preparation time: 20 minutes + 1 hour chilling
Cooking time: 8–10 minutes

230g unsalted butter, softened
170g icing sugar
1 egg
½ tsp. vanilla essence
¼ tsp. peppermint essence
280g plain flour, sifted
¼ tsp. salt
¼ tsp. red food colouring, optional
55g crushed peppermints

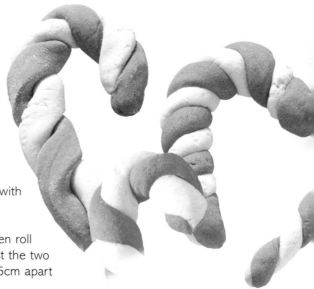

> ### TIP
>
> Food colouring paste is preferable to liquid food colouring. The colour is stronger and it doesn't add liquid to the mixture.

In a large bowl, beat the butter until soft, then beat in the sugar until the mixture becomes light and fluffy. Beat in the egg, vanilla and peppermint essence until combined. Stir in the flour and salt until well blended.

Put half the dough in cling film and seal. Add food colouring and crushed peppermints to the remaining dough and beat until mixed. Wrap tightly in cling film and refrigerate both doughs for 1 hour.

Preheat oven to 180°C (gas mark 4). Grease two baking trays or line with nonstick baking parchment.

To form canes, use a teaspoon to scoop out a piece of plain dough then roll into a 10cm-long log shape. Repeat with the red-coloured dough. Twist the two logs together, and bend the top end to form a cane shape. Set canes 5cm apart on the baking trays.

Bake until firm, about 8–10 minutes; do not let them brown at all. Cool for a few minutes then put on wire racks to cool completely. Store in an airtight container.

Makes about 24

Cranberry and Orange Clusters

The tartness of dried cranberries adds a certain bite to these soft-textured Thanksgiving cookies.

Preparation time: 20 minutes
Cooking time: 15 minutes

115g unsalted butter
90g caster sugar
zest of 1 orange
1 egg
115g rolled oats
75g dried cranberries
150g plain flour
½ tsp. baking powder

TIP

If your dried cranberries have withered, resurrect them by soaking them in warm orange juice until plump. Drain them thoroughly and let cool before using.

Preheat oven to 180°C (gas mark 4). Lightly grease two baking trays or line with nonstick baking parchment.

Beat the butter, sugar and orange zest in a bowl until creamy. Gradually add the egg, beating well between each addition. Stir in the oats and cranberries. Sift the flour and baking powder into the bowl and mix everything until evenly combined.

Put small tablespoons of the mixture on the prepared baking trays, spacing them well apart. Flatten slightly with the back of a fork. Bake for 15 minutes until well raised and light golden brown. Leave on the baking trays for 5 minutes, then transfer to a wire rack to cool. The cookies will still be soft when you take them out of the oven, but will become firm as they cool.

Makes 20

Pumpkin Fingers

These buttery shortcake fingers with a pumpkin topping make a great, portable alternative to pumpkin pie for a Thanksgiving supper.

Preparation time: 30 minutes
Cooking time: 40–45 minutes

115g plain flour
55g icing sugar
60g unsalted butter
1 egg yolk

Topping
2 cups cooked pumpkin
225ml single cream
2 eggs, beaten
225g light brown sugar
1 tsp. ground cinnamon
1 tbsp. icing sugar, for dusting

Preheat oven to 180°C (gas mark 4). Grease a shallow 18 x 28cm tin and line with nonstick baking parchment.

Sift the flour and icing sugar into a bowl. Blend in the butter until the mixture resembles fine bread crumbs. Add the egg yolk and mix to a dough. Lightly knead on a floured surface until smooth, then press into the base of the prepared tin. Prick all over with a fork, then bake for 10 minutes, until golden.

For the filling, sift the cooked pumpkin to make a smooth paste. Stir in the cream, eggs, sugar and cinnamon. Pour over the base and bake for 40–45 minutes more, or until a skewer inserted into the middle comes out clean.

Leave to cool in the tin, then cut into 18 fingers. Remove from the tin and lightly dust with icing sugar before serving.

Makes 18

Halloween Cookies

Cut your cutters out and have a fun-filled afternoon with the kids. Make white ghosts with black eyes, orange pumpkins and black witches. You might want to make up a double batch of dough.

Preparation time: 40 minutes + 30 minutes chilling
Cooking time: 10–12 minutes

115g lightly salted butter
55g caster sugar
zest of 1 lemon
1 egg, beaten
250g plain flour
25g cornflour
½ tsp. vanilla essence
shop-bought coloured icings and decorations

Preheat oven to 180°C (gas mark 4). Lightly grease two baking trays or line with nonstick baking parchment.

Beat the butter, sugar and lemon zest together until pale and fluffy. Gradually add the egg, beating well after each addition. Sift the flour and cornflour together and blend into the butter mixture with the vanilla. Lightly knead for a few seconds until smooth. Wrap in cling film and chill for 30 minutes.

Roll out on a floured surface to 5mm thick, then, using cutters, press out Halloween shapes. Put on the prepared baking trays. Bake the smaller cookies for 10 minutes and the larger ones for 12 minutes, until golden. Leave to cool on the baking trays for 3 minutes, then transfer to a wire rack to cool before decorating with coloured icings and decorations.

Makes 30

4th July Cookies

These giant all-American cookies are coated with icing in the colours of the flag – red, white and blue.

Preparation time: 35 minutes
Cooking time: 15 minutes

60g lightly salted butter
120g shortening
75g light brown sugar
1 egg, beaten
½ tsp. vanilla essence
150g self-raising flour

Icing
170g ready-to-roll fondant icing
red and blue food colouring

TIP

Unbaked, this cookie mixture will keep in a sealed container in the refrigerator for up to a week. However, the cookies are best eaten on the same day that they are iced.

Preheat oven to 190°C (gas mark 5). Lightly grease two baking trays or line with nonstick baking parchment.

Beat the butter, shortening and sugar together until light and fluffy. Gradually add the egg and vanilla, beating well between each addition. Sift the flour and stir into the mixture.

Drop tablespoonfuls of the mixture onto the baking trays, spacing well apart. Flatten to about 2cm thick. Bake for 15 minutes, until golden. Leave on the baking trays for 2–3 minutes, then remove and cool on a wire rack.

Divide the fondant into 3, and colour one part red, one part blue and leave the final part white. Roll each out, and cut strips to decorate your cookies however you like.

Makes 8

Cinnamon Drops

These are very popular Passover cookies, as they contain no flour.

Preparation time: 20 minutes
Cooking time: 25–30 minutes

230g blanched and ground almonds, walnuts or pecans
150g caster sugar
1 tbsp. ground cinnamon
2 egg whites
¼ tsp. cream of tartar
scant 115g icing sugar
1 tbsp. ground cinnamon

TIP

These flour-free morsels make great celebration cookies for anyone on a gluten-free diet.

Preheat oven to 325°F. Grease or line two baking trays with nonstick baking parchment.

In a medium bowl, combine the nuts, half the sugar and the cinnamon. In a separate bowl, beat the egg whites until foamy. Add the cream of tartar, and continue beating until soft peaks form. Gradually add the remaining sugar, a tablespoon at a time, beating well after each addition, until the whites are stiff and glossy. Gently fold in the nut mixture.

With moistened hands, shape the mixture into walnut-sized drops. Put on baking trays 3cm apart. Bake until set and golden for 25–30 minutes, turning the baking trays halfway through cooking. Let the cookies cool slightly.

Combine the icing sugar and cinnamon. Roll each warm cinnamon drop in the mixture to coat completely, then set on a wire rack to cool. Roll drops in the cinnamon-sugar again when cold. Store in an airtight container.

Makes about 20

Hanukkah Sugar Cookies

Search out some unusual cutters for this special joyous holiday, or make your own Jewish star template from a piece of cardboard.

**Preparation time: 45 minutes + at least
 2 hours chilling
Cooking time: 20–4 minutes**

250g plain flour
½ tsp. baking powder
½ tsp. salt
170g unsalted butter, softened
140g caster sugar
1 egg, beaten
zest of 1 lemon
1 tbsp. fresh lemon juice

1 tsp. vanilla essence
½ tsp. lemon essence

Icing
500g icing sugar
2–3 tbsp. milk
1 tbsp. lemon juice
food colouring

> **TIP**
>
> To save time on the big day, the dough can be made up to two days ahead and left wrapped and ready in the refrigerator.

Into a medium bowl, sift together the flour, baking powder and salt. In a large bowl, beat the butter, until creamy, then add the sugar and beat until light and fluffy. Gradually beat in the egg, lemon zest and juice, vanilla and lemon essence until well blended. Little by little add the flour mixture until a soft dough forms. Wrap in cling film and refrigerate for several hours or overnight until firm enough to roll.

Preheat oven to 180°C (gas mark 4). Grease or line two baking trays with nonstick baking parchment.

On a lightly floured surface, roll out half the dough to 5mm thick (keep the remaining dough refrigerated). Using a floured cutter or template, cut out as many shapes as possible. Put 3cm apart on the baking trays. Bake until golden, 10–12 minutes. Let the cookies cool slightly, then transfer to wire racks to cool completely. Repeat with the remaining dough.

In a medium bowl, sift the icing sugar. Stir in 2 tablespoons of milk and the lemon juice, adding a little more milk if the mixture is too thick. Add a few drops of food colouring, mixing to the desired shade. Spoon the icing into a piping bag and pipe designs or decorations onto each cookie shape. Leave icing to set for 2 hours. Store in an airtight container with a layer of greaseproof paper between each of the cookie layers.

Makes about 40

Honeyed Hearts

These honey cookies with a crunchy sugar topping will melt even the hardest heart.

Preparation time: 20 minutes + 30 minutes chilling
Cooking time: 15 minutes

85g lightly salted butter
55g caster sugar
1 tbsp. creamed honey
1 egg, beaten
170g plain flour
2 tbsp. cornflour
1 tbsp. egg white
2 tbsp. brown sugar coffee crystals

TIP

Dust flour underneath the dough if it shows any signs of sticking to the work surface at all; flour that rolling pin too!

Preheat oven to 180°C (gas mark 4). Lightly grease two baking trays or line with nonstick baking parchment.

Beat the butter, sugar and honey until very soft, light and fluffy. Gradually add the egg. Sift the flour and cornflour together and work into the butter mixture to make a soft dough. Lightly knead on a floured surface for a few seconds until smooth, then wrap in cling film and chill in the refrigerator for 30 minutes.

Roll out on a lightly floured surface to 5mm thick. Cut into heart shapes using a 5cm cutter, then transfer these to the baking trays, spacing them slightly apart. Brush the cookies with egg white and sprinkle each with a few sugar crystals. Bake for 15 minutes, or until lightly browned. Leave the cookies on the baking trays for 2–3 minutes, then remove and cool on a wire rack.

Makes 30

Rose Petal Cookies

Make these fragrant cookies using red or yellow perfumed rose petals.

Preparation time: 25 minutes + 1 hour chilling
Cooking time: 8–10 minutes

250g plain flour
115g icing sugar
200g unsalted butter
petals of 2 roses

TIP

Make sure that you use unsprayed and freshly picked roses for these cookies.

Lightly grease two baking trays or line with nonstick baking parchment. Sift the flour and icing sugar into a bowl. Blend in the butter until the mixture resembles fine bread crumbs.

Snip the rose petals into small pieces with scissors and stir into the mixture. Continue to blend with the fingers until a dough forms. Lightly knead for a few seconds on a floured surface until smooth. Roll the dough into a cylinder about 20cm long. Wrap in cling film and chill in the refrigerator for 1 hour.

Preheat oven to 325°F. Cut the dough into 1cm slices and arrange on the baking trays, spacing slightly apart. Bake for 8–10 minutes, until light golden brown. Leave on the baking trays for 2 minutes, then remove and cool on a wire rack.

Makes 16

Soft Centres

A crisp coffee case conceals a melted chocolate centre. Serve these cookies when freshly baked and still warm.

Preparation time: 25 minutes + 20 minutes chilling
Cooking time: 10 minutes

140g unsalted butter
150g caster sugar
2 tsp. coffee essence
1 egg yolk
280g self-raising flour
55g plain chocolate
55g white chocolate
1 tbsp. unsweetened cocoa powder, for dusting

TIP

These create a wow factor if you serve them for dessert. Put the prepared cookies on the baking tray in the refrigerator until 15 minutes before serving, then pop them in the oven when ready.

Lightly grease a large baking tray or line with nonstick baking parchment.

Beat the butter and sugar until light and fluffy. Beat in the coffee essence and egg yolk. Sift the flour into the bowl and mix to a firm dough. Wrap and chill in the refrigerator for 20 minutes.

Preheat oven to 180°C (gas mark 4).

Roll out about a third of the dough on a lightly floured surface to 2mm thick and cut out 20 circles with a 5cm cutter. Transfer to the prepared baking tray. Put a square of chocolate in the middle of each circle. Roll out the remaining dough and cut out 20 circles with a 6cm cutter. Lay these over the chocolate-topped bases, pressing the edges together to seal and enclose the filling.

Bake for 10 minutes, until darkened and risen. Leave on the baking trays for 5 minutes, then remove and cool on a wire rack. Dust with cocoa powder before serving.

Makes 20

Shamrocks

The emblem of Ireland is the shamrock and these cookies are ideal to serve on St Patrick's Day.

Preparation time: 25 minutes + 30 minutes chilling
Cooking time: 15 minutes

55g mint-flavoured chocolate sticks
170g butter
200g caster sugar
1 egg
350g plain flour

Icing
225g icing sugar
¼ tsp. mint essence
2 tbsp. hot water
green food colouring

TIP

Instead of icing, brush the surface of the uncooked cookies with a little beaten egg white, then sprinkle with mint-flavoured sugar (available in cake decorating shops) or green-coloured sugar.

Lightly grease two baking trays or line with nonstick baking parchment.

Finely chop the mint-flavoured chocolate sticks. Beat the butter and sugar until light and fluffy. Gradually add the egg, beating well after each addition. Sift the flour into the bowl, add the chocolate pieces and mix to a soft dough. Lightly knead for a few seconds until smooth, then wrap in cling film and chill in the refrigerator for 30 minutes.

Preheat oven to 180°C (gas mark 4). Roll out the dough on a lightly floured surface to 5mm thick and cut into shamrock shapes with a 6cm cutter. Transfer to the baking trays. Bake for 15 minutes, until light golden brown. Leave on the baking trays for 2–3 minutes, then remove and cool on a wire rack.

Sift the icing sugar into a bowl. Add the mint essence and enough water to make a thick icing. Stir in a drop of green food colouring. Use to ice the cookies. Leave the icing to set before serving.

Makes 20

Sedgemoor Easter Cookies

Legend tells that when the Duke of Monmouth was fleeing the Battle of Sedgemoor, he fell into a ditch. A local woman thought he was an unfortunate peasant down on his luck and baked him these cookies.

Preparation time: 15 minutes
Cooking time: 20 minutes

225g plain flour
1 tsp. ground cinnamon
115g lightly salted butter
55g caster sugar
75g currants
1 egg, beaten
2 tbsp. brandy
1 tbsp. milk
1 tbsp. granulated sugar, for sprinkling

Preheat oven to 180°C (gas mark 4). Lightly grease two baking trays or line with nonstick baking parchment.

Sift the flour and cinnamon into a bowl and blend in the butter until the mixture resembles bread crumbs. Stir in the sugar and currants. Mix the egg, brandy and milk together and stir into the dry mixture to produce a soft dropping consistency.

Drop tablespoonfuls of the mixture onto the baking trays and sprinkle with granulated sugar. Bake for 20 minutes, until lightly browned and firm. Leave on the baking trays for a few minutes, then remove and cool on a wire rack.

Makes 16

> **TIP**
> Many English towns have variations on this cookie, often including the addition of lemon zest.

Easter Egg Cookies

These chocolate, chocolate chip cookies with pastel ribbon and bow icing make great Easter treats.

Preparation time: 25 minutes
Cooking time: 15 minutes

60g butter
200g caster sugar
1 egg, beaten
315g plain flour
25g unsweetened cocoa powder
2 tbsp. cornflour
⅓ cup plain chocolate chips

Icing
225g icing sugar
2 tbsp. hot water
pink, blue and yellow food colouring

TIP
White chocolate chips or toffee chips could be substituted for the plain chocolate chips for a lighter colour and sweeter flavour.

Preheat oven to 180°C (gas mark 4). Lightly grease two baking trays or line with nonstick baking parchment.

Beat the butter and sugar until light and fluffy. Gradually add the egg. Sift the flour and cocoa with the cornflour and work into the butter mixture with the chocolate chips to make a stiff dough. Lightly knead the dough for a few seconds until smooth.

Roll out on a floured surface to a thickness of 5mm. Cut into 20 ovals with a plain or fluted 8cm oval cutter. Bake in the oven for 15 minutes, until firm to the touch. Leave the cookies to cool on the baking trays for a few minutes, then remove to a wire rack to cool completely.

For the icing, sift the icing sugar into a bowl and stir in enough hot water to make a smooth icing. Divide the icing into three and colour one pale pink, one pale blue and one pale yellow. Spoon into piping bags, snip off the ends and pipe a ribbon and bow design on each cookie in your chosen colours. Leave to set before serving.

Makes 20

Fruity Cookies

The fresh and dried fruits in these cookies give them a taste-tingling array of flavours to awaken your senses and send you into another realm of being.

Fruity Cookies

This wonderful chapter is a collection of good old favourites mixed with some unusual cookies that take advantage of the exciting range of fabulous fruits that are now available in our supermarkets. Everyday fruits such as apples, oranges and bananas make an appearance alongside exotic passionfruit and mangos.

Some recipes use fresh fruit while others exploit the rich, intense flavours of dried fruit. The Passion Fruit Shortcake uses fresh fruit with panache, while the recipe for Dried Mango and Ginger Delights provides the perfect vehicle for flavoursome dried fruits. A number of cookies contrast the sharp flavour of the fruit with the sweetness of the cookie for stunning effect; the Truly Blueberry Cookies and the Tangerine Bars are two such treats to savour.

There are several bar cookies in this section; the Spicy Mixed Fruit Bars would be fantastic to discover in a lunchbox, and many of the other chunky fruit cookies travel well. Next time you plan a camping trip, or take a day at the beach, make up a batch of Pear and Walnut Cookies or some Rum and Raisin Cookies to eat when the hunger pangs strike.

Date and Cinnamon Cookies

Dates are soft and chewy and keep these cookies really moist.

Preparation time: 15 minutes + 2 hours chilling
Cooking time: 15–18 minutes

230g butter, softened
170g light brown sugar
3 tbsp golden syrup
2 eggs, beaten
350g plain flour
1 tsp ground cinnamon
260g chopped dates

Put the butter, sugar and golden syrup in a bowl. Beat until light and fluffy. Gradually add the eggs, mixing well between additions. Sift in the flour and cinnamon and mix well. Stir in the dates. Chill for 2 hours.

Preheat oven to 180°C (gas mark 4). Grease two baking trays or line with nonstick baking parchment.

Roll teaspoons of the mixture into balls and flatten slightly. Arrange on the baking trays at least 5cm apart and bake for 15–18 minutes. Let cool for 5 minutes then transfer to wire racks to cool completely. Store in an airtight container.

Makes about 30

TIP

Avoid over-mixing drop cookies when preparing. This limits the aeration of the dough, which helps to keep cookies from inflating in the oven and falling flat when you take them out.

Orange and Cardamom Thins

These are delicate sandwich cookies, but they are also great fun for kids to make.

Preparation time: 40 minutes + 30 minutes chilling
Cooking time: 12 minutes

115g butter, softened
140g caster sugar
2 medium eggs, beaten
zest of 1 large orange
115g plain flour
2 tsp ground cardamom

Put the butter and sugar in a bowl and beat until light and fluffy. Gradually beat in the eggs and orange zest. Sift in the flour and ground cardamom and mix well. Form into a ball, wrap in plastic and chill for 30 minutes.

Meanwhile, beat together the filling ingredients, adding the orange juice gradually.

Preheat oven to 190°C (gas mark 5). Grease two baking trays or line with nonstick baking parchment.

Roll out the dough thinly and cut out triangles with a sharp knife. Put the cookies on the baking trays, spaced about 3cm apart. Bake for about 12 minutes until golden. Cool for 5 minutes on the sheet then transfer to wire racks to cool completely.

Makes about 20

Spicy Mixed Fruit Bars

These are substantial bars of moist fruit and coconut –
well worth the effort.

Preparation time: 30 minutes
Cooking time: 35–45 minutes

Topping
50g finely chopped dried apricots
50g sultanas
50g finely chopped dried peaches
50g dried blueberries
3 tbsp brandy
3 eggs, beaten
115g light brown sugar
55g plain flour
1 tsp baking powder
40g dessicated coconut

Base
120g butter, softened
70g caster sugar
150g plain flour
1 tsp ground ginger
1 tsp ground cinnamon

Put the apricots, sultanas, peaches and blueberries in a bowl and add the
brandy. Leave to soak for 20 minutes.

Preheat oven to 180°C (gas mark 4). Grease and line the base of a 33 x
23cm tin with nonstick baking parchment.

Prepare the base. Put the butter and sugar in a bowl and beat
until light and fluffy. Sift in the flour, ginger and cinnamon and
mix to a dough. Spread over the base of the pan and bake for
8–10 minutes.

While the base is cooking, finish making the topping. Beat the
eggs and sugar together for about 5 minutes until thick and
creamy. Sift in the flour and baking powder. Stir in the coconut and
soaked fruit. Pour over the baked base and bake for a further 30–5
minutes until firm to the touch. Cool in the tin before cutting into
12 bars. Store in an airtight container.

Makes 12

Cherry and Vanilla Squares

Use dried Morello or sour cherries, rather than glacé cherries for these moist squares.

Preparation time: 20 minutes
Cooking time: 30–35 minutes

150g plain flour
40g icing sugar
200g cold butter
2 tsp vanilla essence
225g dried cherries

Preheat oven to 180°C (gas mark 4). Grease or line a 20 x 20cm tin with nonstick baking parchment.

Sift the flour and icing sugar together into a bowl. Add the butter and vanilla and blend in with your fingertips until the mixture resembles coarse bread crumbs. Stir in the cherries and form into a soft dough.

Transfer to the tin and press to fit. Bake for 30–35 minutes. Leave to cool then cut into 16 squares. Store, covered in the tin or in an airtight container.

Makes 16

Carrot and Date Drops

These are unusual, delicious and moist – maybe more like a cake than a cookie.

Preparation time: 15 minutes + 2 hours chilling
Cooking time: 10–12 minutes

115g butter, softened
115g light brown sugar
1 egg, beaten
90g plain flour
1 tsp baking powder

1 tsp salt
1 tsp ground nutmeg
½ tsp ground ginger
¾ cup grated carrot
175g chopped dates

TIP

For texture you could use pecans instead of dates, although the resulting cookies will be less sweet.

Put butter and sugar in a bowl and beat until light and fluffy. Gradually beat in the egg. Sift in the flour, baking powder, salt, nutmeg and ginger and stir until combined. Then stir in the carrots and dates. Refrigerate for at least 2 hours.

Preheat oven to 190°C (gas mark 5). Grease two baking trays or line with nonstick baking parchment.

Take small tablespoons of the mixture and roll into balls, then flatten slightly. Put at least 5cm apart on the baking trays and bake for 10–12 minutes. Cool for 5 minutes on the baking trays then transfer to wire racks to cool completely. Store the cookies in an airtight container.

Makes about 25

Passionfruit Shortcake

Sometimes called purple granadillas, passionfruits contain masses of small seeds that are left in the dough for an added crunch.

TIP

If you don't like the passionfruit seeds, pass the flesh through a non-reactive sieve before using it.

Preparation time: 25 minutes + 1 hour chilling
Cooking time: 20 minutes

170g butter, softened
50g caster sugar
170g plain flour
55g cornflour
pulp of 3 passionfruits
icing sugar to decorate, optional

Put butter and sugar in a bowl and beat until light and fluffy. Sift in the flour and cornflour and mix to a dough by hand. Stir in the passionfruit pulp.

Transfer to a piece of greaseproof paper, wrap up, then chill for at least 1 hour in the refrigerator.

Preheat oven to 180°C (gas mark 4). Grease two baking trays or line with nonstick baking parchment.

Roll out the dough to about 1cm thick and cut out shapes using a heart-shaped cutter. Put these onto the baking trays and bake for about 20 minutes until golden brown. Cool for 5 minutes on the baking trays then transfer to wire racks to cool completely. Dust with icing sugar to serve, if desired. Store in an airtight container and eat within four days.

Makes about 20

Dried Mango and Ginger Delights

Using cream cheese makes this cookie dough really soft and pliable.

Preparation time: 20 minutes + 30 minutes chilling
Cooking time: 15 minutes

85g butter, softened
70g cream cheese, softened
140g caster sugar
1 tsp baking powder
1 egg, beaten
1 tbsp ginger preserve or stem ginger syrup
250g plain flour
175g finely chopped dried mango
2 tsp finely chopped candied or stem ginger

TIP

Make a double batch of the base for this cookie, then freeze half before adding the mango and ginger. You can then flavour the reserved dough with different fruit combinations next time.

Put butter and cream cheese in a bowl and beat for 30 seconds. Add sugar and beat until light and fluffy. Add the baking powder, egg and syrup and beat again. Sift in the flour and beat for 30 seconds.

Stir in the mango and chopped stem or preserved ginger and form the mixture into a soft dough. Form into a ball, wrap in cling film and chill for 30 minutes in the refrigerator.

Preheat oven to 180°C (gas mark 4). Grease two baking trays or line with nonstick baking parchment.

Roll out the dough to just under 1cm thick and stamp out stars with a cutter. Re-roll as necessary. Transfer to the baking trays and bake for about 15 minutes until lightly golden. Cool for 5 minutes on the baking trays then transfer to wire cooling racks. Store the cookies in an airtight container.

Makes about 40

Cherry Chocolate Cookies

Chunky and chewy – great feel-good cookies!

Preparation time: 20 minutes + 2 hours chilling
Cooking time: 15–18 minutes

140g butter
140g caster sugar
1 egg yolk
200g plain flour
225g roughly chopped glacé cherries
⅔ cup plain chocolate chips

TIP

For a nutty chocolate cherry cookie, use half the quantity of cherries suggested and add ½ cup chopped macadamia nuts.

Put the butter and sugar in a bowl and mix well until light and fluffy. Add the egg yolk and beat. Sift in the flour and mix well, then stir in the cherries and chocolate chips. Chill for at least 2 hours.

Preheat oven to 190°C (gas mark 5). Grease two baking trays or line with nonstick baking parchment.

Take tablespoons of the mixture and roll into balls, then flatten slightly. Put onto the baking trays at least 3cm apart. Bake for 15–18 minutes. Cool for 5 minutes on the baking trays then transfer to wire racks to cool completely. Store in an airtight container.

Makes about 18

Tangerine Bars

Scrumptious shortcake with a tangy tangerine orange topping. This would work well with lemons too.

Preparation time: 30 minutes + chilling
Cooking time: 40–5 minutes

Base
230g butter
70g caster sugar
zest of 1 tangerine orange
225g plain flour
55g cornflour

Topping
zest of 2 tangerine oranges
200g caster sugar
3 eggs, beaten
scant 55g plain flour, sifted
½ tsp baking powder, sifted
3 tbsp freshly squeezed tangerine
   orange juice

Grease a 23 x 33cm tin or line with nonstick baking parchment.

Put the butter, sugar and tangerine zest in a bowl and beat together until light and fluffy. Sift in the flour and cornflour; mix well then form into a soft dough. Press into the prepared tin and smooth with a knife. Chill for 30 minutes in the refrigerator.

Preheat oven to 180°C (gas mark 4). Bake for 15–20 minutes until lightly golden. Remove from the oven, leaving the oven switched on.

Meanwhile, make the topping. Beat together the tangerine zest, sugar and eggs until creamy. Fold in the flour and baking powder. Stir in the tangerine juice. Pour over the shortbread and bake for a further 25 minutes. Cool in the pan. Cut into 30 bars. Dust with icing sugar to serve, if desired.

Makes 30

Cranberry and White Chocolate Cookies

Dried cranberries are not as tart as fresh ones and the cookies are made even sweeter by the addition of chocolate.

Preparation time: 30 minutes + 1 hour chilling
Cooking time: 15–20 minutes

230g butter, softened
150g caster sugar
170g light brown sugar
2 eggs, beaten
250g plain flour

1 tsp salt
1 tsp baking powder
225g dried cranberries
1½ cups white chocolate chips,
    or white chocolate, chopped

> **TIP**
>
> For larger cookies, use an ice-cream scoop to shape your cookies, then flatten slightly with the palm of your hand. But remember to leave more space for spreading.

Beat together the butter and sugars until soft and creamy. Gradually beat in the eggs, adding 1 tablespoon of flour with the second egg if the mixture curdles. Sift in the flour, salt and baking powder and mix to combine. Add cranberries and ⅔ cup of the white chocolate chips and mix well. Chill the mixture for at least 1 hour in the refrigerator.

Preheat oven to 180°C (gas mark 4). Grease two large baking trays or line with nonstick baking parchment.

Roll tablespoons of the mixture into balls and put onto the baking trays, at least 8cm apart. Flatten slightly with the back of a spoon. Bake for 15–20 minutes until golden.

Leave to cool for 5 minutes then transfer to wire racks to cool completely. If desired, melt the remaining white chocolate over a bowl of simmering water, and drizzle it over the cookies. Leave to cool before serving. Store in an airtight container.

Makes about 30

Truly Blueberry Cookies

Macerating (soaking) the blueberries in orange and brandy makes the cookies even moister and more delicious. Omit the brandy and increase the orange juice if you want to make these cookies for kids.

Preparation time: 20 minutes + 1 hour chilling
Cooking time: 15–18 minutes

225g dried blueberries
4 tbsp orange juice
2 tbsp brandy
230g butter, softened
150g caster sugar

170g light brown sugar
2 eggs, beaten
250g plain flour, sifted
1 tsp baking powder, sifted

Put the blueberries, orange juice and brandy in a small pan and simmer for 5 minutes. Remove from the heat and leave to cool. Beat together butter and sugars until soft and creamy. Gradually beat in the eggs, adding 1 tablespoon of flour with the second egg if the mixture curdles.

Stir in the remaining flour and baking powder and mix to combine. Strain the blueberries, discarding any liquid, and add to the cookie mixture. Mix well. Chill the mixture for at least 1 hour in the refrigerator.

Preheat oven to 180°C (gas mark 4). Grease two large baking trays or line with nonstick baking parchment.

Roll tablespoons of the mixture into balls and put on the baking trays, at least 8cm apart. Flatten slightly with the back of a spoon. Bake for 15–18 minutes, until golden. Leave to cool for 5 minutes then transfer to wire racks to cool completely.

Store in an airtight container.

Makes 18

Pear Bars

Dried pears make these cookies all sticky and chewy.

Preparation time: 15 minutes
Cooking time: 20–5 minutes

115g butter
150g soft brown sugar
2 tbsp golden syrup
270g rolled oats
1 cup chopped dried pears
⅓ cup currants

Preheat oven to 190°C (gas mark 5). Lightly grease a shallow 28 x 18cm tin.

Put the butter, sugar and golden syrup in a pan and cook over a gentle heat until the butter has melted. Combine the dry ingredients and add to the pan; stir well.

Spoon into the prepared tin and press down with the back of a spoon. Bake for 20–5 minutes until lightly golden. Cool for 5 minutes in the tin then cut into 16 bars; leave to cool completely in the tin. Store in an airtight container.

Makes 16

TIP

Muscavado sugar, also called Barbados sugar, is minimally processed and results in a toffee-like sweetness. Using this instead would complement the ingredients in this recipe perfectly.

Glacé Cherry Florentines

This is the best recipe to use when you want a quick, but impressive cookie.

Preparation time: 20 minutes
Cooking time: 8–10 minutes

60g lightly salted butter
2 tbsp golden syrup
50g caster sugar
40g plain flour
170g finely chopped glacé cherries
zest of 1 orange
115g dark chocolate

TIP
For an extra-rich cookie, add 2 tbsp double cream with the cherries and orange zest.

Preheat oven to 180°C (gas mark 4). Grease two large baking trays or line with nonstick baking parchment.

Put the butter, golden syrup and sugar in a saucepan over a medium heat and stir until the sugar dissolves. Remove from the heat and cool for 5 minutes, stirring frequently. Sift in the flour, then stir in the cherries and orange zest. Mix well.

Drop heaping teaspoons onto the baking trays, at least 8cm apart. Shape them into neat rounds. Bake for 8–10 minutes. Reshape into rounds while hot, if necessary. Cool for 5 minutes, then transfer to wire racks to cool completely. Melt the chocolate, and dip one side of each cookie. Return to wire rack to set.

Store the cookies in an airtight container.

Makes about 12

Candied Peel and Dark Chocolate Squares

For a special occasion these dark treats are perfect. Make up a batch to put in a gift box and take to a dinner party.

Preparation time: 45 minutes
Cooking time: 25–30 minutes

225g plus 2 tbsp plain flour
50g caster sugar
170g cold butter, cut into small pieces
60g chopped candied peel
120g good-quality plain chocolate

Preheat oven to 180°C (gas mark 4). Grease and line the base of a shallow 28 x 18cm tin.

Sift the flour into a bowl and stir in the sugar. Add the butter and blend in with your fingertips until the mixture resembles coarse bread crumbs. Stir in 30g of the candied peel and form into a soft dough.

Roll out to just under the size of the tin. Transfer to the tin and press to fit. Prick all over with a fork. Bake for 25–30 minutes until lightly browned. Cool for 5 minutes then mark into 24 bars or squares. Cool in the tin.

Melt the chocolate in a microwave or in a bowl over a saucepan of simmering water. Cut the dough into squares and remove from the tin. Dip each one into the chocolate to coat the top and sides and put on greaseproof paper. While the chocolate is still warm, sprinkle over a few pieces of peel. Leave to set before serving. Store in an airtight container with layers of greaseproof paper.

Makes 24

TIP

There is candied peel in the supermarket, then there is candied peel in the specialty food shop. This is often sold in large pieces glazed with sugar. The two don't compare – buy the real thing if you happen to see it, then make these.

Peach Wheels

These wheels are cut from a log of dough filled with a sweet peach filling.

Preparation time: 40 minutes + 50 minutes chilling
Cooking time: 10–12 minutes

Filling
150g dried peaches, finely chopped (see tip)
90g caster sugar
1 tsp ground nutmeg
120ml orange juice

Dough
170g butter, softened
170g light brown sugar
1 medium egg, beaten
1 tsp almond essence
350g plain flour
1 tsp baking powder

TIP

It's important to chop the peaches finely, otherwise it will be difficult when it comes to rolling up the dough.

Put all the filling ingredients in a small saucepan and bring to the boil. Simmer for 3 minutes until most of the orange juice has evaporated and the mixture is thick. Set aside and cool. Put the butter and sugar in a bowl and mix until light and fluffy. Gradually add the egg, mixing well between each addition. Stir in the almond essence. Sift in the flour and baking powder and form into a dough. Wrap in cling film and chill for at least 30 minutes.

Divide the dough in half, then put one half on a piece of floured greaseproof paper. Roll out the dough on the paper to a rectangle 20 x 25cm. Slide a thin metal spatula between the paper and the dough so that it does not stick to the paper when rolled up. Cover the dough with half the filling and roll up from a long side, using the paper to help you roll. Rewrap in cling film and chill for about 20 minutes. Repeat with the remaining dough and filling.

Preheat oven to 180°C (gas mark 4). Grease two baking trays or line with nonstick baking parchment.

Cut 1cm slices from the logs and put onto the baking trays. Bake for 10–12 minutes. Cool on baking trays for 5 minutes then transfer to wire cooling racks. Store in an airtight container.

Makes about 40

Rum and Raisin Cookies

The traditional combination of rum and raisins is perfect for cookies as it makes them moist and chewy.

Preparation time: 20 minutes + 1 hour chilling
Cooking time: 15–17 minutes

230g butter, softened
150g caster sugar
170g light brown sugar
1 egg, beaten
3 tbsp rum
250g plain flour
1 tsp salt
1 tsp baking powder
200g seedless raisins

TIP

Dust your hands with a little flour or icing sugar when forming the dough into balls. This stops the dough from sticking to your hands.

Beat together the butter and sugars until soft and creamy. Gradually beat in the egg and rum, adding 1 tablespoon of flour with the second egg if the mixture curdles. Sift in the flour, salt and baking powder and mix to combine. Add the raisins and mix well. Chill for at least 1 hour in the refrigerator.

Preheat oven to 180°C (gas mark 4). Grease two large baking trays or line with nonstick baking parchment.

Roll tablespoons of the mixture into balls and put on the baking trays at least 8cm apart. Flatten slightly with the back of a spoon. Bake for 15–17 minutes until golden. Leave to cool for 5 minutes then transfer to wire racks to cool completely. Store in an airtight container.

Makes about 35

Brandy and Fresh Apple Cookies

Fresh apples add texture and a sweet flavour.

Preparation time: 20 minutes
Cooking time: 15 minutes

75g grated apple
1 tbsp lemon juice
½ stick butter
2 tbsp golden syrup
50g caster sugar
2 tbsp brandy
55g plain flour
½ cup chopped almonds

TIP

Try using maple syrup instead of the golden syrup for an even richer flavour.

Preheat oven to 180°C (gas mark 4). Grease two large baking trays or line with nonstick baking parchment.

Squeeze the grated apples in your hand to essence the juice. Discard the juice then toss the apple in the lemon juice to coat.

Put the butter, golden syrup, sugar and brandy in a saucepan over a medium heat and stir until the sugar dissolves. Remove from the heat and cool for 5 minutes, stirring frequently. Sift in the flour, then stir in the almonds and apple. Mix well.

Drop heaped teaspoons onto the baking trays, at least 8cm apart. Shape them into neat rounds. Bake for about 15 minutes. Cool for 5 minutes, then transfer to wire racks to cool completely. Store in an airtight container.

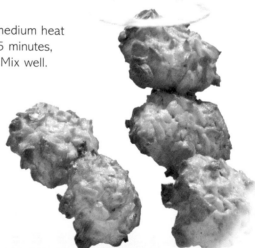

Makes 10–12

Pineapple Drops

These very sweet cookies are complemented by a steaming cup of freshly brewed coffee.

Preparation time: 20 minutes + 1 hour chilling
Cooking time: 15–17 minutes

230g butter, softened
150g caster sugar
170g light brown sugar
2 eggs, beaten
2 tbsp honey

230g plain flour
1 tsp salt
1 tsp baking powder
180g chopped dried pineapple

TIP

To give these cookies a more tropical feel, replace the honey here with 2 tablespoons of coconut liqueur and add 20g of unsweetened dessicated coconut to the mixture.

Put the butter and sugars in a bowl and beat until light and fluffy. Gradually beat in the eggs, adding 1 tablespoon of flour with the second egg if the mixture curdles. Sift in the flour, salt and baking powder and mix. Add the pineapple and mix well. Chill for 1 hour in the refrigerator.

Preheat oven to 180°C (gas mark 4). Grease two large baking trays or line with nonstick baking parchment.

Roll tablespoons of the mixture into balls and put on the baking trays at least 8cm apart. Flatten slightly between your palms. Bake for 15–17 minutes until golden. Leave to cool for 5 minutes then transfer to wire racks to cool completely. Store in an airtight container.

Makes about 30

Pear and Walnut Cookies

These cookies ring the changes and use wholemealflour. This gives the cookies a really rich flavour.

Preparation time: 15 minutes + 1 hour chilling
Cooking time: 15–17 minutes

230g butter, softened
170g light brown sugar
150g caster sugar
2 eggs, beaten
1 tsp vanilla essence

250g wholemeal flour
1 tsp baking powder
1 tsp salt
115g finely chopped dried pears
115g chopped walnut pieces

Put the butter and sugars in a bowl and beat together until pale and creamy. Gradually beat in the eggs and vanilla essence, adding 1 tablespoon of flour with the second egg if the mixture curdles. Sift in the flour, baking powder and salt and mix. Stir in the pears and walnuts and mix well. Chill for at least 1 hour in the refrigerator.

Preheat oven to 180°C (gas mark 4). Grease two baking trays or line with nonstick baking parchment.

Roll tablespoons of the mixture into balls and put onto the baking trays, at least 8cm apart. Flatten with the back of a spoon and top each with a walnut piece, if desired.
Bake for 15–17 minutes until golden, but still soft. Cool for 5 minutes on the baking trays then transfer to wire cooling racks. Store in an airtight container.

Makes about 30

Nutty Cookies

Everyone adores the crispy texture of cookies. Adding nuts intensifies the crunch, making them even more tempting. And if you're a lover of chewy cookies, then you'll appreciate the contrasting bite when they're studded with nuts.

Nutty Cookies

Nuts come in a variety of subtly contrasting tastes and textures and each can be used to best advantage on their own or in clever combinations. Combined with fragrant spices or delectable chocolate, nut-based cookies are simply glorious.

Chunky nuts are a feature in many of the most successful cookies, while others use ground nuts instead of flour, resulting in a cookie with a dense, deep flavour. Try the Pecan and Chocolate Pebbles should you need to be convinced. Anyone fond of a nutty cookie will probably be aware that the latest health findings are in favour of nuts. Nuts are high in proteins, monosaturated fats (the good guys found in olive oil) and masses of micro-nutrients. Of course, these cookies still contain butter and sugar, but hey, everything in moderation.

The following pages are packed with traditional treats and family favourites, such as straight, no-nonsense Peanut Butter Cookies, Coffee and Walnut Cookies and Almond Brittle Cookies. Then there are some clever combinations that exploit nuts paired with other ingredients – the Pistachio and Orange Thins, the Drizzled Chocolate and Brazil Nut Treats and the delectable Double Ginger Pecan Cookies all have an air of sophistication about them and taste divine.

Almond Brittle Cookies

Almond brittle is simple to make and requires no oven, so is perfect for a quick cookie fix.

Preparation time: 25 minutes + 1 hour chilling
Cooking time: 15–20 minutes

170g raw almonds
200g sugar
120ml light golden syrup
1 tsp butter

For the almond brittle, preheat oven to 220°C (gas mark 7). Put almonds on a baking tray and toast for 3–4 minutes. Melt sugar in a small saucepan over medium heat without stirring. Add the almonds, mix quickly, then remove from the heat when mixture is a medium brown colour. Quickly spread onto a baking tray and set in a cool place until it is cool enough to cut into bars with a sharp, greased knife. Do not touch until you're sure it's cool enough: molten sugar carries a lot of heat and will burn fingers easily.

Makes about 20

TIP

Honey Almond Brittle
Simply replace the 90g sugar with 55g runny honey and 50g sugar when making the almond brittle.

Extra-special Peanut Cookies

Sophisticated, and not too sweet, these are the perfect vehicle for some fine dark chocolate.

Preparation time: 20 minutes + 1 hour chilling
Cooking time: 15–18 minutes

230g butter
200g white sugar
1 egg
300g plain flour

1 teaspoon vanilla essence
115g peanuts
2 tbsp caster sugar
170g dark chocolate

TIP

Almost all nuts go well with dark chocolate, so simply substitute your favourite!

In a large bowl, beat together the butter and sugars until soft and creamy. Beat in the egg and then stir in the vanilla. Sift the flour into the butter mixture, and stir until well blended. Cover dough and leave in a cool place for an hour, until firm.

Preheat oven to 180°C (gas mark 4). Grease two baking trays or line with nonstick baking parchment. Roll dough out to 5mm thick, and stamp out circles with a 5cm cutter. Transfer to the baking sheets, and press peanuts into the top of each cookie. Sprinkle with the caster sugar, and bake for 15–18 minutes until golden. Leave to cool for 5 minutes, and then transfer to wire racks to cool completely.

Melt the chocolate, and drizzle lines across the top of each cookie. Leave in a cool place until set. Store in an airtight container for up to one week.

Makes about 25

All-Peanut-Butter Cookies

These are really chunky, perfect for packed lunches and picnics.

Preparation time: 30 minutes + 1 hour chilling
Cooking time: 15–20 minutes

85g butter, softened
⅓ cup crunchy peanut butter
75g dark brown sugar
90g caster sugar
1 egg, beaten
150g plain flour
1 tsp baking powder

TIP

These are the perfect snack to enjoy with a banana milkshake.

Put the butter, peanut butter and sugars in a bowl and beat until light and fluffy. Gradually beat in the egg. Sift in the flour and baking powder. Chill mixture for 1 hour.

Preheat oven to 180°C (gas mark 4). Grease two baking trays or line with nonstick baking parchment.

Put spoonfuls of the dough onto the baking trays, at least 8cm apart. Flatten slightly with the back of a spoon. Bake for 15–20 minutes until golden. Cool for 5 minutes on the baking tray then transfer to wire racks to cool. Store in an airtight container for up to one week.

Makes about 20

Walnut Crescents

These cookies are light, crumbly and nutty.

**Preparation time: 30 minutes + up to
  60 minutes chilling
Cooking time: 20–25 minutes**

115g butter
3 tbsp caster sugar
150g plain flour
½ cup finely chopped walnuts

Put the butter and sugar in a bowl and beat until light and fluffy. Sift in the flour then stir in the walnuts. Mix to form a soft dough. Chill for 30 minutes in the refrigerator.

Grease two baking trays or line with nonstick baking parchment. Dust work surface with a little flour, then roll out dough to just under 1cm thick. Press out crescent shapes with a cutter, re-rolling and pressing out the trimmings. Transfer to the baking trays and, if you have time, chill for a further 30 minutes.

Preheat oven to 170°C (gas mark 3). Bake cookies for 20–25 minutes until lightly golden. Transfer to wire racks to cool. Store in an airtight container for up to one week.

Makes about 25

TIP

These dainty little cookies make the perfect accompaniment to desserts such as lemon mousse, panna cotta or a Mexican-style flan.

Chocolate and Hazelnut Surprises

If you'd rather take a shortcut, shop-bought nut-and-chocolate spread would work for the filling in these moreish cookies.

**Preparation time: 20 minutes +
  overnight chilling
Cooking time: 15–20 minutes**

345g hazelnuts
475ml full-cream milk
4 tbsp powdered milk
3 tbsp runny honey
400g dark or plain chocolate,
  chopped

225g plain flour
230g butter, room temperature
140g sugar
few tablespoons milk, to mix
cocoa powder, to dust

TIP
Triple the quantities of the filling, and store in a jar in the fridge for the most delicious chocolate spread ever!

Preheat oven to 170°C (gas mark 3). Place the hazelnuts on in a baking tin, and bake in oven until golden brown. Remove from oven and let cool before moving to a food processor and processing until very fine. Meanwhile, add the milk, powdered milk and honey to a saucepan and heat until nearly boiling. Remove from the heat and add two-thirds of the processed roasted nuts and all of the chocolate. Allow to melt, stirring to combine. When all mixed in, let cool overnight.

The next day, grease two baking trays or line with nonstick baking parchment. Place the flour and the butter in a large bowl. Rub the butter into the flour until it resembles bread crumbs. Stir in the sugar, and then add enough milk to make a firm dough. Rest in a cool place for 30 minutes. Roll out to 3mm thick, and stamp out circles with a 8cm cutter. Place 1 teaspoon of the filling in the centre, and fold the dough over to make a semi-circle. Press edges together to seal.

Transfer to the baking trays. Bake for 15–20 minutes, until golden. Cool for 5 minutes then transfer to wire racks to cool. Store in an airtight container for up to 2 days.

Makes 24

Pecan and Chocolate Pebbles

These are very rich meringue-style cookies are filled with a delicious chocolate ganache.

Preparation time: 30 minutes
Cooking time: 10–12 minutes

170g pecans
250g caster sugar
3 egg whites
1 tsp vanilla essence

Ganache filling
200g good-quality plain chocolate, broken up
30g unsalted butter
60ml double cream

Preheat oven to 170°C (gas mark 3). Grease two baking trays or line with nonstick baking parchment.

Put pecans in a food processor and grind until finely chopped but not into a paste. Add 200g of the sugar and grind for 10 seconds more.

Beat the egg whites until stiff peaks form. Beat in the remaining sugar a little at a time, beating well after each addition. Beat in the vanilla. Gradually beat in the pecan mixture a little at a time until it is all incorporated.

Fit a piping bag with a 1cm nozzle and fill with the mixture. Pipe 5cm rounds about 3cm apart on the baking trays. Bake for 10–12 minutes until pale golden. Let cool completely on the baking trays before adding the ganache filling.

To make the ganache, melt the chocolate in a bowl in the microwave or over a saucepan of simmering water. Heat the butter and cream in a small saucepan, add to the chocolate and stir until smooth and glossy. Cool, stirring occasionally, until a spreadable consistency is reached. Carefully spread half the meringues with the ganache and sandwich with the remaining meringue. Because these cookies contain fresh cream they should be eaten on the day they are made.

Makes 15

Orange and Macadamia Wafers

Orange flower water gives these cookies a subtle orange flavour resonant of the exotic lands of the eastern Mediterranean.

TIP

Orange flower water is made by soaking bitter orange blossoms in water, then distilling the resulting liquid.

Preparation time: 30 minutes + 60 minutes chilling
Cooking time: 20–5 minutes

115g butter, softened
3 tbsp caster sugar
170g plain flour, plus extra for rolling
¾ cup chopped macadamia nuts
1 tbsp orange flower water
90g good-quality plain chocolate, broken up (optional)

Grease two baking trays or line with nonstick baking parchment.

Put the butter and sugar in a bowl and beat until light and fluffy. Sift in flour, then stir in macadamia nuts and orange flower water. Mix to a soft dough. Chill for 30 minutes.

Dust work surface with a little flour, then roll out dough to just under 1cm thick. Press out small squares with a cutter, re-rolling and stamping out the trimmings. Transfer to the baking trays and chill for at least 30 minutes in the refrigerator.

Preheat oven to 170°C (gas mark 3). Bake cookies for 20–5 minutes until lightly golden. Cool on wire racks.

If desired, add chocolate to the cookies. Melt the chocolate in a bowl in the microwave or over a saucepan of simmering water. Once the cookies have cooled, dip one half of each into the melted chocolate. Put on nonstick paper to set. Store in an airtight container.

Makes 25

Banoffee Squares

These cookies are packed full of chewy banana chips and topped with a rich toffee and pecan sauce – truly scrumptious!

Preparation time: 35 minutes + 30 minutes chilling
Cooking time: 20 minutes

Base
115g butter, softened
90g caster sugar
1 medium egg, beaten
170g plain flour
½ tsp baking powder
scant 1 cup dried banana chips

Topping
60g unsalted butter
170g brown soft sugar
60ml double cream
120ml golden syrup
1¼ cups roughly chopped pecans

> **TIP**
>
> Try to buy banana chips that have been dried without the use of additives. Some chips are dipped in sugar syrup or honey prior to drying.

Grease and line the base and sides of a 28 x 20cm baking tin with nonstick baking parchment.

Put the butter and sugar in a bowl and beat until light and fluffy. Beat in the egg. Sift in the flour and baking powder and mix well. Stir the banana chips into the mixture. Spoon the mixture into the tin, spreading it evenly. This takes a little time and is easiest with a small spatula or blunt knife. Chill for 30 minutes.

Preheat oven to 190°C (gas mark 5). Cover dough with a piece of greaseproof paper and bake for 5 minutes. Remove paper and bake for a further 5 minutes. Cool while making the topping. (Leave the oven turned on.)

To make the topping, put the butter, sugar, cream and golden syrup in a saucepan and melt gently over low heat until the sugar dissolves, stirring frequently. Boil hard for 1 minute. Remove from the heat and stir in the pecans. Pour over the baked crust and bake for a further 10 minutes until the top is bubbling. Leave to cool completely in the pan on a wire rack.

Run a knife around the edges, between the tin and greaseproof paper, and lift out onto a board. Cut into 24 pieces, 6 across and 4 down. Store in an airtight container for up to one week.

Makes 24

Cashew Thins

These cookies are really thin and crunchy – try eating them with ice cream for a delicious treat.

Preparation time: 20 minutes
Cooking time: 8–10 minutes

60g slightly salted butter, softened
55g light brown sugar
60ml golden syrup
½ cup finely chopped salted cashews
40g plain flour
1 tsp vanilla essence
170g white chocolate, coarsely chopped

TIP
Turn the baking tray around halfway through cooking if your oven does not cook evenly.

Preheat oven to 180°C (gas mark 4). Grease two baking trays or line with nonstick baking parchment.

In a saucepan, melt the butter. Add the brown sugar and golden syrup, then bring to the boil, stirring constantly for 3–4 minutes until the sugar dissolves. Remove from the heat. Stir in the cashews, flour and vanilla.

Drop half teaspoonfuls spaced well apart onto the baking tray. Use the back of the spoon to spread each heap into a circle. Bake for 8–10 minutes or until golden brown. Cool on the baking tray for 1 minute, then transfer to a wire rack to cool completely.

Melt the chocolate in a small bowl set over a saucepan of barely simmering water. Dip a fork into the melted chocolate and drizzle over the cookies. Return to cooling rack to set. Once set, store in an airtight container. Not suitable for freezing.

Makes about 30

199

Pistachio and Orange Thins

These are sophisticated little cookies, just perfect with a cup of coffee.

Preparation time: 30 minutes + 30 minutes chilling
Cooking time: 15 minutes

115g butter, softened
3 tbsp caster sugar
3 tbsp light brown sugar
3 tbsp Grand Marnier or orange juice
170g plain flour
115g shelled, unsalted pistachios

Put the butter and sugars in a mixing bowl and beat until pale and creamy. Beat in the Grand Marnier or orange juice. Sift in the flour and mix to a firm dough. Transfer to a piece of greaseproof paper and roll into a log 5cm in diameter. Chill for 30 minutes.

Meanwhile, grind or finely chop the pistachios and transfer to a sheet of greaseproof paper. Roll the log in the pistachios several times, ensuring the whole log is covered in nuts. Rewrap in the greaseproof paper and chill for a further 30 minutes.

Preheat oven to 170°C (gas mark 3). Grease two baking trays or line with nonstick baking parchment.

Cut the log into slices of just under 1cm and put on the baking trays, 5cm apart. Bake for 15 minutes. Cool for 5 minutes then transfer to wire racks to cool. Store in an airtight container for up to 1 week.

Makes about 25

Double Almond Cookies

If you like almonds, you'll love these cookies! You simply couldn't fit any more almonds in the batter.

Preparation time: 15 minutes + 1 hour chilling
Cooking time: 15–17 minutes

230g butter, softened
150g caster sugar
170g light brown sugar
2 eggs, beaten
225g plain flour
1 tsp salt
1 tsp baking powder
1½ cups chopped blanched almonds
115g flaked almonds

TIP

Nuts contain lots of oil and so quickly become rancid if left exposed to air. Store in airtight containers in the refrigerator for four months (sometimes up to a year). If you have nuts left over that you do not plan to use, they will store in the freezer for longer.

Beat together the butter and sugars until soft and creamy. Gradually beat in the eggs, adding 1 tablespoon of the flour if it begins to curdle. Sift in flour, salt and baking powder and mix to combine. Add all the almonds and mix well. Chill mixture for at least 1 hour in the refrigerator.

Preheat oven to 180°C (gas mark 4). Line two large baking trays with nonstick baking parchment.

Roll tablespoons of the mixture into balls and put onto the baking trays at least 8cm apart. Flatten slightly with the back of a spoon. Bake for about 15–17 minutes until golden. Leave to cool for 5 minutes then transfer to wire racks to cool. Store in an airtight container.

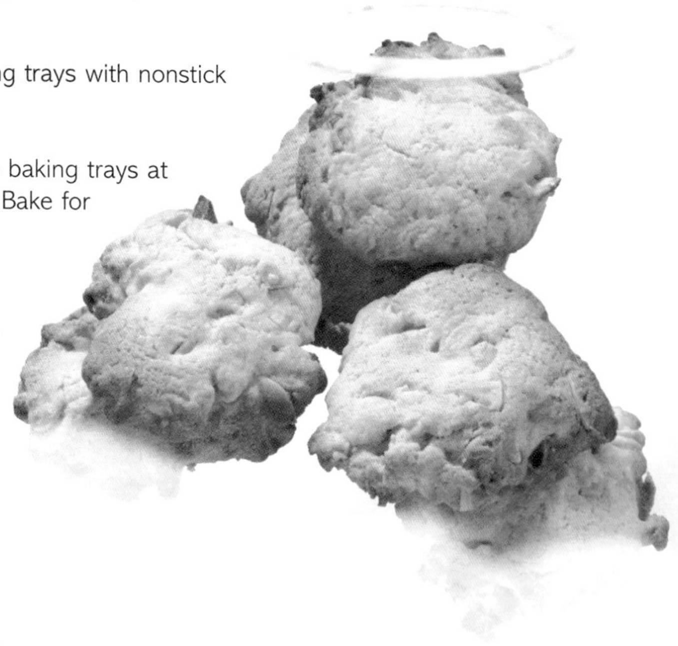

Makes about 30

Drizzled Chocolate & Brazil Nut Treats

The swirled chocolate makes these cookies a bit special.

Preparation time: 35 minutes + 1 hour chilling
Cooking time: 10–15 minutes

230g butter, softened
170g light brown sugar
150g caster sugar
2 eggs, beaten
250g plain flour
1 tsp baking powder
1 tsp salt
1 cup finely chopped Brazil nuts
55g plain chocolate, chopped

TIP

For chewy cookies, remove from the oven when the edges are golden but their centres are still soft and not yet quite cooked through.

Put the butter and sugars in a bowl and beat together until pale and creamy. Gradually beat in the eggs, adding 1 tablespoon of the flour if they begin to curdle. Sift in flour, baking powder and salt and mix. Stir in the Brazil nuts and mix well. Chill for 1 hour.

Preheat oven to 180°C (gas mark 4). Grease two baking trays or line with nonstick baking parchment.

Roll tablespoons of the mixture into balls and put onto the baking trays, at least 8cm apart to allow for speading. Flatten with the back of a spoon. Bake for 10–15 minutes until golden, but still soft. Cool for 5 minutes on the baking trays then transfer the cookies to wire cooling racks.

Melt the chocolate in a microwave or over a saucepan of steaming water. Using a teaspoon, drizzle the chocolate over the cookies. Let set before serving. Best eaten on the day made, but may be stored in an airtight container.

Makes about 25

Coffee and Walnut Cookies

Coffee and walnuts are a classic combination and perfect for a mid-morning snack.

Preparation time: 20 minutes + 1 hour chilling
Cooking time: 15–18 minutes

230g butter, softened
170g light brown sugar
150g caster sugar
2 eggs, beaten
250g plain flour
1 tsp baking powder
1 cup finely chopped walnuts

Frosting
115g icing sugar
2 tsp coffee granules
1 tbsp hot water

TIP

For extra strong coffee flavour, add 1 tablespoon coffee granules with the sugar.

Put the butter and sugar in a bowl and beat until light and fluffy. Gradually beat in the eggs, adding a tablespoon of the flour if they begin to curdle. Sift in flour and baking powder and mix. Stir in the walnuts and mix well. Chill for 1 hour.

Preheat oven to 180°C (gas mark 4). Grease two baking trays or line with nonstick baking parchment.

Roll tablespoons of the mixture into balls and put onto the baking trays, at least 8cm apart. Flatten with the back of a spoon. Bake for 15–18 minutes until golden, but still soft. Cool for 5 minutes on the baking trays then transfer to wire racks.

Sift the icing sugar into a bowl. In a small cup dissolve the coffee in the hot water, then stir into the sugar. Use to decorate the cookies, leave to set. Store in an airtight container for up to one week.

Makes 35

Pine Nut and Lemon Cookies

Toasting pine nuts brings out their flavour and gives them a slightly smoky taste. The glaze is optional.

Preparation time: 15 minutes + 1 hour chilling
Cooking time: 10–15 minutes

⅔ cup pine nuts
115g unsalted butter, softened
225g light brown sugar
200g caster sugar
2 eggs, beaten
zest of 1 lemon
115g, plus 2 tbsp plain flour
1 tsp baking powder
1 tsp salt

Glaze
5 tbsp granulated sugar
2 tbsp water
1 tsbp. lemon juice
zest of 1 orange
rind of 1 lemon

TIP

For a special occasion, omit 1 tablespoon water and stir 1 tablespoon liqueur or rum into the glaze once it has cooled.

Preheat oven to 190°C (gas mark 5). Grease or line two baking trays with nonstick baking parchment.

Put the butter and sugars in a bowl and beat together until pale and creamy. Gradually beat in the eggs, adding 1 tablespoon of the flour should the mixture begin to curdle. Stir in the lemon zest. Sift in the flour, baking powder and salt. Stir in the nuts. Wrap in cling film and chill for 1 hour.

Roll the mixture into walnut-sized balls and put on baking trays, 8cm apart. Flatten slightly with the back of a spoon. Bake until set and golden but still soft, for 10–15 minutes. Cool for 5 minutes, then transfer to a wire rack.

To make the glaze, gently dissolve the sugar in the water and lemon juice with the zest and rind. Boil for 5 minutes, cool, then drizzle a little over each cookie. Eat within 2 days or the glaze will turn the cookies soft.

Makes about 15

Double Ginger Pecan Cookies

These cookies are for real ginger lovers – they contain both ground ginger and stem or preserved ginger.

Preparation time: 20 minutes
Cooking time: 15–20 minutes

200g plain flour
1 tsp baking powder
2 tsp ground ginger
1 tbsp caster sugar
¾ cup chopped pecans
115g butter

120ml golden syrup
1 tbsp finely chopped stem
    ginger or ginger preserve
2 tsp stem ginger syrup or
    additional golden syrup

Preheat oven to 190°C (gas mark 5). Grease two baking trays or line with nonstick baking parchment.

Sift the flour, baking powder and ground ginger into a large bowl. Stir in the sugar and pecans and make a well in the centre.

Put the butter, syrup, stem ginger and stem ginger syrup, if using, in a small saucepan and stir over gentle heat until the butter has melted. Pour into the dry ingredients and mix to a soft dough. Cool for 10 minutes.

Take teaspoons of the mixture and roll into balls. Put on the baking trays at least 5cm apart and flatten slightly with the back of a spoon. Bake for 15–20 minutes, until golden. Cool for 5 minutes then transfer to wire racks. Store in an airtight container for up to one week.

Makes 25

Nuts and Cherry Cookies

Any combination of nuts can be used, or buy a packet of ready-mixed nuts.

Preparation time: 30 minutes + 1 hour chilling
Cooking time: 10–15 minutes

230g butter, softened
115g light brown sugar
150g caster sugar
2 eggs, beaten
250g plain flour
1 tsp baking powder
1 tsp salt
1 cup finely chopped mixed nuts
225g dried Morello or sour cherries

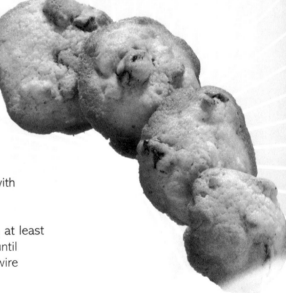

TIP

Chopped dried papaya could be substituted for the cherries for an exotic variation.

Put the butter and sugars in a bowl and beat together until pale and creamy. Gradually beat in the eggs, adding 1 tablespoon of the flour if it begins to curdle. Sift in flour and baking powder and mix. Stir in the chopped nuts and cherries and mix well. Chill for 1 hour.

Preheat oven to 180°C (gas mark 4). Grease two baking trays or line with nonstick baking parchment.

Roll tablespoons of the mixture into balls and put onto the baking trays, at least 8cm apart. Flatten with the back of a spoon. Bake for 10–15 minutes until golden, but still soft. Cool for 5 minutes on the sheets then transfer to wire cooling racks.

These cookies are best eaten on the day they are made, but may be stored in an airtight container for slightly longer.

Makes 30

Pecan and Marshmallow Cookies

These chewy cookies are simply irresistible! The marshmallows melt in little patches of each cookie giving an unexpected burst of flavour.

Preparation time: 15 minutes + 1 hour chilling
Cooking time: 10–15 minutes

340g butter, softened
115g light brown sugar
150g caster sugar
2 eggs, beaten
3 tbsp clear honey
250g plain flour
1 tsp baking powder
1 tsp salt
1 cup finely chopped pecans
2 cups mini marshmallows

TIP

These are great cookies to take camping or to keep up your energy on a long walk.

Put the butter and sugars in a bowl and beat together until pale and creamy. Gradually beat in the eggs and honey. Sift in the flour, baking powder and salt; mix well. Stir in the pecans and marshmallows until well combined. Chill for at least 1 hour.

Preheat oven to 180°C (gas mark 4). Grease two baking trays or line with nonstick baking parchment.

Roll tablespoons of the mixture into balls and put onto the baking trays, at least 8cm apart. Flatten with the back of a spoon. Bake for 10–15 minutes until golden, but still soft. Cool for 5 minutes on the baking trays then transfer to wire racks. Store in an airtight container for up to one week.

Makes about 25

Walnut and Marmalade

Adding marmalade to cookies gives them a toffee-like flavour and texture.

Preparation time: 15 minutes + 1 hour chilling
Cooking time: 15–18 minutes

230g butter, softened
170g light brown sugar
150g caster sugar
2 eggs, beaten
70g orange marmalade
250g plain flour
1 tsp baking powder
1 tsp salt
1 cup finely chopped walnuts

TIP

With a large glass of milk, a couple of these cookies would make a great start to the day.

Put the butter and sugars in a bowl and beat together until pale and creamy. Gradually beat in the eggs and marmalade. Sift in the flour, baking powder and salt and mix. Stir in the walnuts and mix well. Chill for 1 hour.

Preheat oven to 180°C (gas mark 4). Grease two baking trays or line with nonstick baking parchment.

Roll tablespoons of the mixture into balls and put onto the baking trays, at least 8cm apart. Flatten with the back of a spoon. Bake for 15–18 minutes until golden, but still soft. Cool for 5 minutes on the baking trays then transfer to wire racks. Store in an airtight container for up to one week.

Makes about 30

Walnut and Carrot Cookies

Carrots have a sweet flavour and make the perfect match for walnuts.

Preparation time: 30 minutes + 1 hour chilling
Cooking time: 10–12 minutes

170g butter, softened
200g, plus 2 tbsp caster sugar
2 eggs, beaten
1¼ cups chopped walnuts
⅔ cup shredded carrot
375g plain flour
1 tsp baking powder

TIP

Use a medium grater or microplane for the carrots. If you use a larger gauge, the carrot pieces will be too large to cook through properly.

Put butter and sugar in a mixing bowl and beat until pale and fluffy. Gradually beat in the eggs. Stir in the walnuts and shredded carrot. Sift in the flour and baking powder and form into a dough. Chill for 1 hour.

Preheat oven to 180°C (gas mark 4). Grease two baking trays or line with nonstick baking parchment.

Take tablespoonfuls of the dough and form into balls. Put on the baking trays at least 3cm apart and flatten with the back of a spoon. Bake for 10–12 minutes. Cool on the baking trays. Store the cookies in an airtight container.

Makes about 20

Bar Cookies

Bar cookies are an ingenious cross between a cookie and a cake and come in a whole spectrum of flavours. Not only do they look tantalising on a plate, but wrap them in paper and you can graze on them anywhere, anytime.

Bar Cookies

Bar cookies are cookies baked in a tin, like a brownie, and cut into slices. Almost any drop cookie recipe can be adapted to fit in a tin and, hey presto, you end up with a delicious bar that can be baked in one go: cookies without the batch cooking. It's no wonder that they have become so popular.

Bar cookies are sure to please everyone in the family. Hikers love them – imagine how good biting into a tangy Fig and Oat Slice would be when the hunger pangs kick in; school kids adore them – finding a Rocky Road Pizza or a Toffee Bar wrapped up in their lunchbox brings squeals of delight; while late-risers might rely on finding a Fruit and Nut Bar thrust into their hands on the way out the door. There is even a Grasmere Gingerbread to please Grandma's memories of simplicity.

Versatility is another characteristic of the bar cookie that has secured its popularity. The Spanish Date Slices or the Double Chocolate and Mango Brownies could grace any dessert table; the Chocolate and Orange Slices or the Linzer Bake are perfect with a cup of tea. And when is not the right time for the lemon bar lover to satisfy their cravings with the extra-special Lemon Cheesecake Bars that are included in this chapter?

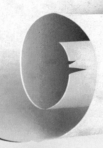

Grasmere Gingerbread

Grasmere, one of the prettiest lakes in the Lake District, is famous for a ginger shortbread. The gingerbread shop in Grasmere jealously guards its recipe but this family recipe is as good, if not better!

Preparation time: 20 minutes
Cooking time: 25–30 minutes

115g lightly salted butter
170g light brown sugar
1 tbsp golden syrup
225g plain flour
1½ teaspoons ground ginger
1 tbsp chopped candied orange peel or citrus peel
1 tbsp chopped candied ginger
2 tbsp icing sugar, optional

Preheat oven to 180°C (gas mark 4). Grease and base-line a 18 x 28cm shallow tin and line with greaseproof paper or nonstick baking parchment.

Beat the butter, sugar and golden syrup until light and well blended. Mix in the remaining ingredients and press into the prepared tin.

Bake for 25–30 minutes or until pale golden. Cut into 16 pieces while still hot but leave in the tin to cool. Dust with icing sugar, if desired. Store in an airtight container.

Makes 16

> **TIP**
> Try to find candied orange peel rather than candied citrus peel because the flavour and texture is superior.

Coconut Slices

This recipe is a delicious mixture of basic store cupboard ingredients.

Preparation time: 3 hours
Cooking time: 15–20 minutes

Base
115g butter
50g sugar
5 tbsp. cocoa powder
1 egg
1 tsp. vanilla extract
12 digestive biscuits, crushed
75g dessicated coconut
125g walnuts

Filling
75g butter
3 tbsp. vanilla custard powder
60ml milk
400g confectioners' sugar

icing sugar

Topping
225g dark chocolate
2 tbsp. butter

Grease and base-line an 20 x 28cm tin.

Melt the butter in a saucepan, and stir in the sugar and cocoa powder. Remove from heat, and whisk in the egg and vanilla extract. Stir in the biscuit crumbs, coconut, and walnuts. Press into the prepared tin, and chill in the refrigerator for 20 minutes.

While the base is chilling, make the filling. In a medium bowl, beat the butter until creamy, and then beat in the custard powder, milk and sugar. Spread over the base layer and chill in the refrigerator for at least an hour or until set.

Melt the chocolate and remaining butter in a small pan and stir until smooth. Pour over the filling layer and chill until the chocolate begins to harden. Score the chocolate into bars, and chill until completely set.

Cut into 18 bars with a hot knife. Store in an airtight container in the refrigerator for up to a week.

Makes 18

Boston Brownies

Brownies are quite irresistible gooey squares of chocolate heaven and crunchy nuts. This recipe uses only cocoa, which gives it a rich, full flavor—and is useful when the chocolate has disappeared from the cupboard.

Preparation time: 20 minutes
Cooking time: 25–30 minutes

⅔ cup unsweetened cocoa powder
5 tbsp. water
¾ stick margarine or lightly salted butter
2 eggs
1 cup granulated sugar
¾ cup all-purpose flour
¾ cup rough-chopped pecan nuts

TIP

To avoid overcooking, cook the brownies just until they begin to pull away from the sides of the pan.

Preheat oven to 350°F. Grease and base-line an 8 x 8-inch pan.

Put the cocoa in a small saucepan and gradually blend in the water. Briefly stir over a low heat to make a smooth paste. Add the butter or margarine and heat until it has melted.

Beat the eggs and sugar until light and fluffy, then beat in the cocoa mixture.

Sift the flour and fold in, then stir in the nuts. Spread in the pan.

Bake for 25–30 minutes until raised and firm around the edges and the center is set. It is normal for the mixture to sink a little in the center on cooling. Cool for 15 minutes, then cut into 9 large squares. Store in an airtight container.

Makes 9

Rocky Road Pizza

The rocky road cookie appears in many guises. In this version, a very traditional, lemon-flavoured cookie mixture is used to make a pizza base.

TIP

You can use the remaining dough from this to make a few small cookies.

Preparation time: 40 minutes
Cooking time: 30 minutes

Base
225g plain flour
115g lightly salted butter or
    margarine
90g caster sugar
zest of 1 lemon
1 egg
milk, if required

Topping
¼ cup mixed chopped nuts
1¼ cups mini marshmallows
½ cup milk or plain chocolate chips
2 tbsp caramel topping

Preheat oven to 180°C (gas mark 4). Grease or line a baking tray with nonstick baking parchment.

Prepare the pizza base. Sift the flour into a bowl and blend in the butter or margarine to make fine bread crumbs. Stir in the sugar and lemon zest. Beat the egg and use it, together with milk if needed, to make a firm but soft dough. It must not be sticky.

To make an 20cm base, roll the dough out into a circle. Lift onto the baking tray and use a tart ring or plate as a guide to the correct shape. Alternatively, use a pizza pan.

Bake for about 20 minutes until pale golden and cooked in the centre. Five minutes before the end of the cooking time, put the mixed chopped nuts on a baking tray and slip into the oven to toast. Leave there for about 10 minutes, until just starting to colour.

Allow the pizza base to cool slightly, then scatter the marshmallows over the surface, followed by the nuts and the chocolate chips. Drizzle the caramel topping over and return to the oven for about 10 minutes until the pizza edges are a deeper colour and the marshmallows are just starting to melt. Serve hot or cold.

Makes 8 wedges

Chocolate and Raspberry Macaroon Bars

These are small, rich bars with an intense chocolate flavour. Use home-cooked or good-quality raspberry jam, if possible, because its flavour mingles deliciously with the chocolate.

Preparation time: 25 minutes
Cooking time: 25–35 minutes

Base
90g plain flour
40g unsweetened cocoa powder
85g lightly salted butter
2 egg yolks
3 tbsp caster sugar
4–5 tbsp good-quality raspberry
  jam

Topping
90g caster sugar
90g ground almonds
1½ tbsp ground rice
2 egg whites
3 drops almond essence
1½ tsp unsweetened cocoa powder

TIP
For a coconut variation, use 60g sweetened dessicated coconut instead of ground almonds.

Preheat oven to 180°C (gas mark 4). Grease and base-line a 18 x 28cm tin.

For the shortcake base, sift the flour and cocoa, blend in the butter and stir in the egg yolks and sugar. Work together to form a dough and press into the tin. Lightly spread the raspberry jam over the shortcake.

Put the sugar, ground almonds and ground rice in a bowl and gently mix. Whisk the egg white and almond essence until it stands in stiff peaks. Gradually fold in the dry ingredients to a stiff mixture. Spoon over the jam and spread roughly with a fork dipped in water.

Bake for 25–35 minutes until dry but not coloured. Mark into pieces while still warm and then leave in the tin until cold. Lightly dust with sifted cocoa powder. Store in an airtight container.

Makes 25

Chocolate and Orange Slices

These easy slices are another example of the versatility of rolled oats.

Preparation time: 30 minutes
Cooking time: 15–20 minutes

115g margarine
115g plain flour
½ tsp bicarbonate of soda
1 tbsp unsweetened cocoa powder
230g oatmeal
50g caster sugar

Topping
3 tbsp icing sugar
1 tsp unsweetened cocoa powder
zest and juice of ½ an orange
candied orange pieces, to decorate

TIP

The orange flavour is only in the icing, so make sure that it tastes strong enough before you pour it on. If in doubt, add a little more orange zest.

Preheat oven to 180°C (gas mark 4). Grease and base-line an 20 x 20cm tin.

Melt the margarine gently in a large saucepan. Sift the flour, baking powder and cocoa and stir into the margarine along with the oatmeal and sugar.

Press into the tin and level the surface. Bake for 15–20 minutes until shrinking from the sides of the pan. Cool while preparing the topping.

Sift the icing sugar and cocoa together and mix with sufficient orange juice to make a thin icing. Stir in the orange zest and pour over the cookies while still warm. It will look more like a glaze than a thick icing.
Cut into 12 slices and decorate each one with a small piece of candied orange, if desired.

Makes 12

Cranberry and Sultana Bars

Cranberries give a vivid colour and sharp flavour in contrast to the sweet base mixture. They are most widely available in the autumn, but freeze well, so can often be bought frozen.

TIP

Frozen cranberries may be used for this recipe, as long as they are free-flowing.

Preparation time: 20 minutes
Cooking time: 25–35 minutes

115g margarine or butter
115g soft brown sugar
2 eggs, beaten
115g self-raising flour
25g ground almonds
115g cranberries
100g sultanas

Preheat oven to 180°C (gas mark 4). Grease and base-line an 20 x 20cm tin.

Beat the margarine and sugar until light and fluffy. Beat in the eggs gradually. Sift the flour and gently fold in, together with the ground almonds, whole cranberries and sultanas.

Pour into the tin and bake for 25–35 minutes until light to the touch, firm in the centre and shrinking slightly from the sides of the tin. Turn out onto a wire rack to cool, then cut into 16 slices. These bars are best stored in the refrigerator or in a cool place.

Makes 16

Easy Apricot Squares

These are very easy – only five ingredients are quickly combined into a soft, succulent bar. Do leave the apricots in large pieces to make the squares more chewy.

Preparation time: 15 minutes
Cooking time: 20–30 minutes

60g lightly salted butter
3 tbsp creamed honey
3 tbsp golden syrup
¾ cup dried apricots, halved
300g muesli

Preheat oven to 160°C (gas mark 3). Grease and base-line an 20 x 20cm tin.

Soften the butter, beat until light, then beat in the honey and syrup. Stir in the remaining ingredients thoroughly and press into the tin. Bake for 20–30 minutes. Cool for 5 minutes, then cut into 9 squares. Leave to cool completely before removing from the tin. Store in an airtight container.

Makes 9

> **TIP**
>
> For a spicy apricot square, add 1 teaspoon ground ginger or cinnamon with the other ingredients.

Double Chocolate and Mango Brownies

A luscious brownie with white chocolate pieces inside. The mango contrasts well with the traditional rich chocolate and pecan mixture. This version is firmer than the other brownie recipes, to hold all these exciting textures.

Preparation time: 30 minutes
Cooking time: 25–30 minutes

115g plain chocolate
60g lightly salted butter
2 eggs
115g packed soft brown sugar
115g self-raising flour
½ cup chopped candied mango
½ cup chopped pecan nuts
⅓ cup white chocolate chips
⅓ cup plain chocolate chips
icing sugar, for dusting

> **TIP**
>
> If this isn't chocolatey enough, add a layer of melted plain chocolate over the cooled brownies and sprinkle over additional chopped dried mango.

Preheat oven to 190°C (gas mark 5). Grease and base-line an 20 x 20cm tin.

Melt the chocolate over a bowl of hot water or in the microwave for 1½–2 minutes. Slice the butter into the chocolate and stir to melt, reheating briefly if necessary.

Beat the eggs and sugar until thick and stir into the chocolate mixture. Beat again, then gently fold in the flour, mango, nuts and two types of chocolate chips. Pour the mixture into the tin. Bake for 25–30 minutes or until the centre appears set and stable. Cool in the tin and cut into 12 pieces, then dust with icing sugar.

Makes 12

Fig and Oat Slices

· ·

This is a useful and economical recipe. It freezes well for up to three months. It is a welcome addition to lunchboxes and may be served warm with yoghurt for a winter dessert.

TIP

Try to find unwaxed lemons, oranges and limes when using citrus zests, as even a good wash does not remove all the wax from the skins.

Preparation time: 20 minutes
Cooking time: 30–5 minutes

1 cup figs
5 tbsp water
zest of ½ orange
170g wholemeal flour
180g rolled oats
75g soft brown sugar
170g margarine

Preheat oven to 180°C (gas mark 4). Grease and base-line an 20 x 20cm tin.

Chop the figs, discarding the stalks, and put in a pan with the water and orange zest. Bring to the boil and simmer for 5 minutes until very soft.

Mix the flour and oats in a large bowl. Melt the sugar and margarine gently and stir into the oat mixture. Thoroughly combine and press half into the tin. Level the top and press well in.

Spread the fig mixture on top and cover with the remaining oat mixture, levelling and pressing it as much as possible. Bake for 30–5 minutes until golden and the mixture is shrinking from the sides of the tin. Cool, cut into 12 slices, and store in an airtight container.

Makes 12

Brazil Nut Blondies

Blondies are brownies without the chocolate. To fill the flavour gap there are plenty of nuts in this sweet, chewy bar.

Preparation time: 15 minutes
Cooking time: 15–20 minutes

1 egg
340g dark brown sugar
1 tsp vanilla essence
90g plain flour
¼ tsp bicarbonate of soda
1 cup chopped Brazil nuts
2 tsp milk
dried cranberries

Preheat oven to 180°C (gas mark 4). Grease and base-line a 20 x 20cm shallow tin.

Beat the egg and stir in the sugar and vanilla essence. Sift the flour and bicarbonate of soda into the mixture and mix in together with the nuts and milk. The mixture will be very thick.

Spread into the tin and bake for 15–20 minutes until set. Mark into 12 squares before completely cold, then leave to cool in the tin. Store in an airtight container.

Makes 12

TIP

The dark brown sugar gives these bars their dark colour and caramel flavour. Alternatively, you can use caster sugar for a lighter, less dense blondie.

Fruit and Brandy Sticks

This recipe is an excellent way of preserving leftover fruit cake. If much of it is still remaining in the cake tin after New Year, use some of it up in this recipe, and freeze.

Preparation time: 30 minutes

1½ cups fruit cake crumbs
60g lightly salted butter
2 tbsp golden syrup
55g plain chocolate
1 tbsp brandy

Icing
6 tbsp icing sugar
rose water or water
pink food colouring

Grease an 20 x 20cm tin and then line the base of the pan as well.

Put the cake crumbs into a bowl and chop any large pieces of fruit or nuts. Melt the butter, syrup and chocolate very gently and combine with the cake crumbs and brandy.

Press into the pan. Level and firm the mixture and chill for at least a day before completing. The cookies may be frozen at this stage.

Remove the mixture from the pan and put on a board. To make the icing, sift the icing sugar and mix to a thick consistency with sufficient water and/or rose water to make a thin icing. However, add the rose water cautiously and taste the strength before use and mix with water if too strong. Add a drop or two of pink food colouring, beat well and add a few drops more water if the icing is too stiff. Pour evenly over the cake. Alternatively, you could frost the mixture with melted chocolate.

Before the icing sets completely, cut into 25 thin fingers with a sharp knife dipped into hot water. Allow to dry before storing the pieces in an airtight container.

Makes 25

Lemon Cheesecake Bars

These fingers would be excellent taken on a summer picnic to round off a sumptuous meal with friends. The cream cheese makes them a little more substantial to withstand any knocks en route.

TIP

Use lime instead of lemon for an even more zingy flavour.

Preparation time: 50 minutes
Cooking time: 50 minutes

Base
170g plain flour
85g margarine or lightly salted butter
1 egg, separated
1 tbsp water

Topping
225g, plus 2 tbsp cream cheese
1 egg, separated
90g caster sugar
zest and juice of 1 lemon
1 tbsp plain flour
50g sultanas
1 tbsp rum, optional

Preheat oven to 190°C (gas mark 5). Grease then base- and side-line a 18 x 28cm shallow tin.

Make the pastry by lightly blending the margarine or butter into the flour. Beat together the egg yolk (reserve the white for cheesecake mixture) and water, add to the mixture to make a soft dough. Use a little more water if necessary as the dough must be pliable. Reserve one quarter of the pastry. Roll out the remaining pastry and line the base of the tin. Press a piece of foil on top of the pastry. Bake for about 20 minutes. Remove the foil and cool. Increase the oven temperature to 200°C (gas mark 6).

Beat the cream cheese, egg yolk, sugar, lemon zest and juice to thoroughly combine and stir in flour, sultanas and rum, if using. Beat the 2 egg whites to a firm peak and beat 2 tablespoons into the cheese mixture, then fold in the rest. Pour over the cooled pastry base and level gently.

Roll out the remaining pastry and cut into shapes to decorate the top. Bake for 15 minutes, reduce the temperature to 180°C (gas mark 4), then bake for 15 minutes longer. Cool in the tin and cut into bars. Store in an airtight container in the refrigerator for 2–3 days.

Makes 12

Turtle Bars

If you have not tried turtle bars, you need to! This combination of flavours is divine.

Preparation time: 45 minutes
Cooking time: 30–35 minutes

Base	Topping
Base	**Topping**
175g butter	115g butter
60g sugar	150g light brown sugar
1 tsp. vanilla extract	125g dark chocolate chips
200g plain flour	
225g pecan halves	

> **TIP**
> Add a shot of strong espresso to the topping mix before pouring over the base for a turtle with a twist!

Preheat oven to 190°C (gas mark 5). Grease then base- and side-line a 18 x 28cm shallow tin with aluminium foil.

Cut the butter into chunks and melt in a saucepan over a gentle heat. Remove from the heat and stir in the sugar and vanilla. Stir in the sifted flour. Press the dough into the bottom of the prepared pan, and bake for 10 minutes. Remove from oven, scatter over the pecans, and bake for 10 minutes more until the crust is golden. Remove from the oven.

To make the topping, melt the butter and stir in the sugar. Bring the mixture to a boil and boil for 1 minute. Pour the hot butter mixture over the base. Bake for 10 minutes then remove from the oven and sprinkle over the chocolate chips. Lift the foil and transfer to a chopping board. Cut into bars. Store in an airtight container for 5 to 7 days.

Makes 24

Linzer Bake

Linzer Torte is a traditional Austrian dessert of raspberries and a light, spiced pastry, which is a cross between cake and pastry. This version would be perfect to pack for a special picnic.

Preparation time: 40 minutes + 30 minutes chilling
Cooking time: 25–30 minutes

170g self-raising flour
½ tsp ground cloves
½ tsp mixed spice
5 tbsp lightly salted butter
90g caster sugar
40g ground almonds or hazelnuts

zest of ½ lemon
1 egg
½ tsp vanilla essence
1-2 tbsp milk
1½ cups raspberry jam

Preheat oven to 180°C (gas mark 4). Meanwhile, grease and base-line an 20 x 20cm shallow tin or dish.

Sift the flour and spices and blend in the butter. Stir in the sugar, ground almonds and lemon zest. Beat together the egg and vanilla essence and stir in, followed by sufficient milk to make up to a firm but slightly soft dough. Gently knead to remove any cracks, wrap in plastic and chill for 30 minutes.

Roll out the pastry and use to line the tin. Trim the pastry level with the top of the tin. Fill the centre with raspberry jam.

Roll out the trimmings and cut into lattice strips. Put two or three in each direction over the jam to make an even lattice. Do not try weaving the strips as this pastry is too fragile.

Bake in the oven for 25–30 minutes until the pastry is barely coloured.

Makes 9 dessert portions

Spanish Date Slices

This traditional recipe uses a delicious combination of dates and oranges.

Preparation time: 45 minutes
Cooking time: 40 minutes

Base
60g lightly salted butter or
   margarine
2 tbsp caster sugar
1 tbsp beaten egg
zest of ½ an orange
115g plain flour

Filling
1 cup pitted dates
1 tbsp rum or orange juice
55g ground almonds
2 tbsp cornflour
70g caster sugar
3 egg whites

Preheat oven to 180°C (gas mark 4). Grease and base-line a 18 x 28cm shallow tin.

Make the pastry base. Beat the butter or margarine and sugar together until light and fluffy. Beat in the egg and orange zest, then work in the flour. Press into the base of the tin.

Chop the dates and pour over the rum or orange juice. Mix the ground almonds, cornflour and sugar.

Beat the egg whites to a stiff peak, then fold in the soaked dates and dry ingredients. Spread over the pastry. Bake for about 40 minutes or until the centre is firm. Leave to cool in the tin, then cut into 16 slices. Store in an airtight container.

Makes 16

Toffee Bars

These bars are known by a multitude of recipe names but the three layers of shortbread, caramel and chocolate are universally popular with people of all ages.

Preparation time: 45 minutes
Cooking time: 20 minutes

Base
115g lightly salted butter
50g caster sugar
150g plain flour

Filling
115g lightly salted butter
200g caster sugar
250ml evaporated milk
few drops vanilla essence

Topping
2 tbsp unsalted butter
85g plain chocolate

TIP
You could also use a 400g tin of ready-made dulce de leche for the filling.

Preheat oven to 180°C (gas mark 4). Grease and base-line a 18 x 28cm shallow tin.

Make the base by beating the butter and sugar together until light, then working in the flour. Press the dough into the tin and bake for 20 minutes or until firm in the centre and lightly golden. Cool in the tin.

Put the butter, sugar and evaporated milk into a heavy-bottomed saucepan and stir over a gentle heat until the sugar has dissolved. Bring to the boil and, stirring constantly, cook for about 15 minutes until thick and caramel in colour. Remove from the heat, beat in the vanilla and pour over the shortbread. Allow to cool.

Gently melt the butter and chocolate together. Pour over the caramel and cut into pieces when set. Store in an airtight container.

Makes 16

Cocktail Cookies

These savoury cookies are marvellous for entertaining – little morsels full of surprises, be they crunchy or chewy, rich or spicy, light as a feather or densely satisfying.

Cocktail Cookies

The techniques of cookie making are extended
to include cookies that don't depend on sugar
for their appeal. Instead they use the rich and
appetising flavours of cheese, the mellowness
of nuts and the piquant appeal of spices.
These cookies often contain elements of taste-
tantalising surprise, such as little flecks of ham
or anchovy, or the crackling crunch of seeds, to
ensure that the cookies, once tasted, are eaten
with relish and delight.

Some are brightly flavoured and crunchy, such as
the Parmesan, Paprika Crisps and the Smoked
Cheese Twists, while others are soft and tender,
like the luscious Smoked Salmon and Lemon
Kisses or the Smoked Ham Rings, which can be
sandwiched together for a more substantial snack.

Serve them as finger food for parties – the
Anchovy, Olive & Basil Spirals are a matchless
accompaniment to a glass of chilled white wine,
while the Mixed Nut Clusters with Cajun Spices
go very well with a margarita. Take Roast Pepper
Cookies on picnics, slip Potato and Chilli Bean
Corn Cakes in a lunchbox and offer freshly baked
Herb Crackers with the cheeseboard. You won't be
lost for opportunities to show off these awesome,
but often neglected, baked treats.

Parmesan & Paprika Crisps

These thin, nutty, cheese morsels are delicious served as a snack on their own or to accompany a fine wine.

Preparation time: 15 minutes
Cooking time: 10 minutes

7 tbsp lightly salted butter or margarine
70g flaked almonds
55g ground almonds
75g freshly grated Parmesan cheese
¼ tsp cayenne pepper
1 tsp paprika

TIP

Try Swiss Gruyère cheese in place of the Parmesan – it has a nutty flavour that really shines through in baked goods.

Preheat oven to 180°C (gas mark 4). Line three baking trays with greaseproof paper or baking parchment.

Melt the butter or margarine in a small saucepan. Remove from the heat and stir in the flaked almonds and ground almonds. Stir in the Parmesan cheese, cayenne pepper and paprika.

Drop the mixture, well spaced apart, in 18 small, well-rounded heaps onto the baking trays. Bake in the oven for 10 minutes until golden brown. Remove from the oven and push around the edges of the cookies with the blade of a knife to neaten the shape. Leave on the sheets to cool completely. Carefully lift off using a thin metal spatula. Store between sheets of greaseproof paper in an airtight container for 3–4 days, or freeze in the same way for up to three months.

Makes 18

Quattro Formaggi

Just like the familiar pizza topping, these cookies are flavoured with four different cheeses.

Preparation time: 20 minutes
Cooking time: 20–5 minutes

1 tbsp freshly grated Parmesan cheese
1 tbsp crumbled blue cheese such as
   Roquefort, Danish or Stilton
1 tbsp grated Swiss or Edam cheese
1 tbsp grated mature Cheddar cheese
115g plain flour
pinch of salt
115g lightly salted butter or margarine,
   softened
1 tsp dried oregano

TIP

These cookies turn mum's chicken soup or gran's minestrone into a wholesome meal.

Preheat oven to 180°C (gas mark 4). Grease or line two baking trays with nonstick baking parchment.

Mix all the cheeses together and sift in the flour and salt. Make a well in the centre, and add the butter or margarine and oregano. Using your fingertips blend the mixture together, and shape it into a soft dough.

Divide into 15 walnut-sized balls and put on baking trays, spaced about 5cm apart. Flatten slightly with a fork, and bake for 20–5 minutes until lightly golden and firm to the touch. Cool on the sheets. Best served slightly warmed. Store in an airtight container for 3–4 days, or freeze for up to three months.

Makes 15

Smoked Cheese Twists

Long, thin twisting pastries are just the thing for parties.

Preparation time: 25 minutes + 30 minutes chilling
Cooking time: 20 minutes

5 tbsp lightly salted butter or margarine, softened
3 tbsp full-fat soft cheese
1 egg yolk
170g plain flour
pinch of salt
2 garlic cloves, crushed
75g finely grated smoked cheese
2 tbsp cold water

In a bowl, beat the butter or margarine with the soft cheese and egg yolk.
Sift in the flour and salt. Add the garlic, 40g of the smoked cheese and 2
tablespoons cold water. Stir the mixture to bring the dough together. Turn on to a
lightly floured surface and knead lightly to form a smooth dough. Wrap and chill
for 30 minutes.

Preheat oven to 180°C (gas mark 4). Line two baking trays with nonstick
baking parchment.

Roll out the dough to 5mm thick, and cut into
1cm-wide strips, about 15cm long. Twist the strips
and put onto the baking trays, pressing down the
edges well to prevent them untwisting. Sprinkle lightly
with the remaining cheese. Bake for about 20 minutes
until lightly golden. Transfer to wire racks and cool for
about 15 minutes before serving. Cool completely and put in
an airtight container for one week.

Makes 30

> **TIP**
> Serve these with a sour
> cream and onion dip
> or a fruity pineapple
> cream cheese dip.

Oat Clusters with Cheese Crumble Top

Easy to make and delicious, these crackers have a crisp and chewy texture, with a lightly spiced topping.

Preparation time: 20 minutes
Cooking time: 20 minutes

170g lightly salted butter or
  margarine
180g rolled oats
115g wholemeal flour
1 tsp salt

Topping
1 tbsp freshly grated Parmesan
  cheese
6 tbsp wholemeal flour
30g lightly salted butter or
  margarine
1 tsp cumin seeds, crushed
1 tsp dried thyme

TIP

For a tangy blue cheese variation, use 2 tablespoons of crumbled blue cheese in place of the Parmesan cheese and leave out the cumin seeds.

Preheat oven to 190°C (gas mark 5). Grease or line two baking trays with nonstick baking parchment.

Melt the butter or margarine for the cookies in a saucepan. Remove from the heat and stir in the oats, flour and salt. Set aside.

Now make the crumble. Mix the cheese and flour together and blend in the butter or margarine until well mixed and resembling large fresh bread crumbs.

Drop the oat mixture onto baking trays to form 18 walnut-sized heaps. Space them about 3cm apart. Press them down lightly with a fork and then sprinkle each with a little of the crumble topping, a few cumin seeds and some thyme. Bake in the oven for 20 minutes, until rich golden brown. Leave to cool on the baking trays. Store in airtight containers between sheets of greaseproof paper for up to one week.

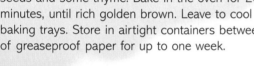

Makes 18

Smoked Ham Rings

These cookies are good to serve with dips, or try sandwiching them together with cream cheese.

Preparation time: 20 minutes
Cooking time: 20 minutes

170g butter or margarine, softened
55g lean smoked ham, very finely chopped
¼ cup finely grated smoked cheese
115g plain flour
55g cornflour
pinch of salt
½ tsp dry mustard powder

TIP

Smoked Fish Rings
Substitute smoked salmon bits for the chopped ham.

Preheat oven to 180°C (gas mark 4). Line two cookie sheets with greaseproof paper or nonstick baking parchment.

In a bowl, beat the butter or margarine, ham and cheese together until well mixed. Sift the remaining ingredients into the bowl and mix well.

Put the dough in a piping bag fitted with a 1cm plain nozzle. Pipe 24 6cm rings, spaced well apart, onto the baking trays. Bake in the oven for 20 minutes until lightly golden. Cool for 5 minutes then transfer to a wire rack to cool completely. Store in an airtight container for up to four days or freeze for up to three months.

Makes 24

Halloumi Cookies

Halloumi cheese is mild tasting, slightly salty and perfect for baking as it holds its shape well.

Preparation time: 15 minutes
Cooking time: 20–25 minutes

115g plain flour
85g Halloumi cheese, cut into small pieces
¼ cup pitted black olives, drained and chopped
2 tbsp freshly chopped coriander
5 tbsp good-quality olive oil

Preheat oven to 180˚C (gas mark 4). Grease or line a large baking tray with nonstick baking parchment.

Sift the flour into a bowl and mix in the cheese, olives and coriander. Bind together with the olive oil to form a dough. Turn onto a lightly floured surface and knead gently until smooth.

Using a teaspoon, pile 14 small heaps onto the baking tray, and press down lightly using a fork. Bake in the oven for 20–25 minutes until lightly golden and firm. Cool for 10 minutes, then transfer to a wire rack. These are best served slightly warmed.

Makes 14

> **TIP**
>
> Recreate the Mediterranean atmosphere by serving these in the early evening with a glass of chilled light beer. If you want to make a meal of it, make a Greek-style salad to go with them.

Crispy Bacon and Blue Cheese Melts

Basic cookie dough is transformed into a melting mixture by adding cheese. Serve these tasty snacks as an accompaniment to other cheeses and fruits, soups and salads.

Preparation time: 25 minutes
Cooking time: 20–25 minutes

6 slices rindless bacon
½ cup crumbled blue cheese
115g plain flour
115g lightly salted butter or margarine, softened
pinch of cayenne pepper

> **TIP**
>
> For a tasty vegetarian option, omit the bacon and add ⅓ cup chopped walnuts as well as ½ teaspoon chopped dried rosemary.

Preheat oven to 180°C (gas mark 4). Grease or line two baking trays with nonstick baking parchment.

Preheat the grill to a hot setting and cook the bacon for 2–3 minutes on each side until golden and crispy. Drain on kitchen towel and allow to cool. Then mince or chop finely.

Mix all the ingredients and the chopped bacon together using a round-bladed knife, and bring together with your hands to form a dough.

Divide the dough into 15 portions and shape each one into a small diamond or disc. Prick the surfaces with a fork and bake in the oven for 20–25 minutes until lightly golden and firm to the touch. Leave to cool for 15 minutes and then serve warm. Store in an airtight container for up to four days.

Makes 15

Pepperoni and Peppercorn Shortcakes

You can make and freeze these tasty pre-dinner nibbles ahead of time, and you may want to double the recipe as they will be very popular.

Preparation time: 15 minutes + 20 minutes chilling
Cooking time: 20–5 minutes

115g plain flour
pinch of salt
115g unsalted butter
55g sliced pepperoni sausage, finely chopped
1 tbsp pickled green peppercorns, drained
1 egg, beaten
freshly ground black pepper

Sift the flour and salt into a bowl, then blend in the butter until you have fine crumbs. Stir in the pepperoni and peppercorns, and add enough egg to bring together to form a dough; reserve the rest for glazing.

Turn onto a lightly floured surface and knead until smooth. Wrap and chill for 20 minutes.

Preheat oven to 160˚C (gas mark 3). Line two baking trays with greaseproof paper or nonstick baking parchment.

Roll out to 5mm thick. Using a 4cm round cutter, stamp out 14 rounds, re-rolling as necessary. Transfer to the baking tray, brush with reserved egg and then dust with a little ground black pepper. Bake in the oven for 20–25 minutes until firm to the touch and golden. Cool for 5 minutes and then transfer to a wire rack to cool completely. To make ahead, pack into an airtight container and freeze for up to three months.

Makes 14

Anchovy, Olive & Basil Spirals

A sophisticated puff pastry snack with a delicious fishy flavour. They are best eaten on the day they are made, and served slightly warmed.

Preparation time: 20 minutes
Cooking time: 10–12 minutes

170g puff pastry, thawed if frozen
1 egg, beaten
55g anchovy fillets, drained
¼ cup pitted black olives, chopped fine
¼ cup pimiento stuffed green olives, chopped fine
15g fresh basil leaves

TIP

Prepare these snacks ahead of time and leave them on baking trays in the refrigerator in a cool place. Pop them into the oven as your first guests arrive.

Preheat oven to 220°C (gas mark 7). Line two baking trays with greaseproof paper or nonstick baking parchment.

Roll out the pastry on a lightly floured surface to a 30 x 20cm rectangle. Brush the pastry with beaten egg and lay the anchovy fillets, lengthwise, over the pastry. Sprinkle with the olives and lay the basil leaves on top. Starting from the long side, roll up the pastry tightly, like a Swiss roll. Press lightly to seal the end, and then slice into 24 pieces.

Lay the pastry pieces, spaced a little apart, on the baking trays, and brush with more egg. Bake for 10–12 minutes until golden and crisp. Cool for 10 minutes before serving. These are best eaten on the day they are made, and served slightly warmed.

Makes 24

Smoked Salmon and Lemon Kisses

These delicately flavoured melt-in-the-mouth soft-bake cookies are good served with cream cheese. This recipe would work well with ham instead of the salmon, if preferred.

Preparation time: 20 minutes
Cooking time: 20–25 minutes

115g plain flour
pinch of salt
2 tbsp freshly chopped parsley
115g smoked salmon pieces, finely grated
½ tsp finely grated lemon zest
115g lightly salted butter or margarine, softened

Preheat oven to 180°C (gas mark 4). Grease or line two baking trays with nonstick baking parchment.

Sift the flour and salt into a bowl. Stir in the parsley, smoked salmon, lemon zest and butter or margarine using a round-bladed knife. Bring together with the hands to form a dough.

Divide the dough into 12 pieces and form them into walnut-sized balls. Put onto baking trays, spaced about 5cm apart. Flatten slightly and bake for 20–25 minutes until lightly golden and firm to the touch. Leave to cool on the baking trays for 15 minutes. These are best served slightly warm, and on the same day as baking. These cookies can be frozen, once baked and cooled, for up to three months.

Makes 12

> **TIP**
>
> For a lemon cream cheese filling mix 115g cream cheese with 1 tablespoon lemon juice, 1 tablespoon fresh chopped dill and a little finely ground black pepper.

Mixed Nut Clusters with Cajun Spices

These cookies are for the real nut lover and are a fantastic drinks party appetiser. They are high in protein, so wouldn't go amiss in a lunchbox either.

Preparation time: 20 minutes
Cooking time: 20–25 minutes

3 tbsp walnut pieces
3 tbsp flaked almonds
3 tbsp macadamia nuts, lightly crushed
3 tbsp shelled unsalted pistachios, lightly crushed
115g plain flour
pinch of celery salt
pinch of onion salt
1 tsp paprika
¼ tsp cayenne pepper
1 tsp dried thyme
115g lightly salted butter or margarine, softened

Preheat oven to 180˚C (gas mark 4). Grease or line two baking trays with nonstick baking parchment.

Mix all the nuts together and put in a bowl. Sift in the flour, salts, paprika and cayenne pepper. Add the thyme and the butter or margarine, and mix together with a round bladed knife. Bring together with your hands to form a dough.

Divide into 15 and form into walnut-sized balls. Put onto baking trays, spaced about 5cm apart. Flatten slightly, and bake in the oven for 20–25 minutes until lightly golden and firm to the touch. Leave to cool on the sheets. These are excellent served slightly warm. Store in an airtight container for up to one week, or freeze for up to three months.

Makes 15

Roasted Pecan Snacks

Use ready-roasted pecan halves in this recipe for a more intense flavour. Try experimenting with honey roast or barbecue smoke-flavoured pecans as an alternative.

TIP

These would also be delicious made with roasted cashew nuts.

Preparation time: 30 minutes + 30 minutes chilling
Cooking time: 20–25 minutes

225g self-raising flour
1 tsp salt
60g lightly salted butter or margarine
7–8 tbsp cold water
scant ⅔ cup roasted pecan nuts, chopped fine

Sift the flour and salt into a bowl and blend in the butter or margarine. Add sufficient water to form a pliable dough. Turn onto a lightly floured surface and knead until smooth.

Roll into a 38 x 15cm rectangle. Mark lightly into three equal portions, and sprinkle the middle portion with one third of the nuts. Fold up the bottom third, bring the top third down over it, seal the edges and give the pastry a half turn. Repeat this rolling and folding twice more, sprinkling with the nuts each time. Re-roll and fold once more. Wrap and chill for 30 minutes.

Preheat oven to 180˚C (gas mark 4). Grease and flour a baking tray.

Roll out the pastry thinly and evenly to form a square slightly bigger than 30cm. Trim away the edges to neaten, and then cut into 1 x 15cm thin fingers; you should make about 24 fingers. Transfer to the baking tray, prick all over with a fork and bake for 20–25 minutes until lightly golden and puffed up. Transfer to a wire rack to cool. Store in an airtight container for up to one week.

Makes 24

Mixed Seed Crunchies

Use small seeds in this recipe to give a very crisp texture. The oats in this recipe add a healthy taste, making them an ideal wholesome snack. Seeds are also great for providing fibre.

Preparation time: 10 minutes + 1 hour standing
Cooking time: 15 minutes

120g rolled oats
70g medium oatmeal
2 tbsp poppy seeds
2 tbsp sesame seeds
1 tsp celery seeds

1 tsp fennel seeds, lightly crushed
120ml sunflower oil
1 tsp salt
1 egg, beaten

TIP

Take these to a football game or use as a school match snack – they're so much better for the kids than fat-laden potato crisps!

Put the oats, oatmeal and seeds in a bowl, and mix in the oil. Leave to stand for 1 hour.

Preheat oven to 160°C (gas mark 3). Line a baking tray with greaseproof paper or nonstick baking parchment.

Add the salt and egg to the oat mixture and beat together thoroughly. Put 18 teaspoonfuls of the mixture, spaced a little apart on a baking tray lined with greaseproof paper and press flat with a wetted fork. Bake in the oven for about 15 minutes until golden brown. Leave to cool on the sheets. Store in an airtight container for up to one week.

Makes 18

Roasted Pepper Cookies

These colorful cookies use three different colored peppers, but you can use just one or two varieties if you prefer.

Preparation time: 25 minutes
Cooking time: 20 minutes

½ small red pepper, seeded
½ small orange pepper, seeded
½ small green pepper, seeded
115g plain flour
pinch of salt
½ tsp hot chilli powder
115g lightly salted butter or margarine, softened
2 tsp dried chilli flakes, optional

TIP

Use a good-quality vegan margarine for these and please your vegan friends.

Preheat the grill to a high setting and put the peppers on the rack. Cook them for 5 minutes on each side until softened and lightly charred. Cool for 10 minutes. Peel if preferred, and then chop the flesh finely. Allow this to cool completely.

Preheat oven to 180˚C (gas mark 4). Grease or line two baking trays with nonstick baking parchment.

Sift the flour, salt and chilli powder into a bowl. Stir in the peppers and butter or margarine. Using a round-bladed knife, mix to form a dough. Divide into 12, and form into walnut-sized balls. Put onto the prepared baking trays, spaced about 5cm apart. Flatten slightly and sprinkle each with a few chilli flakes, if using. Bake in the oven for 20 minutes until lightly golden and firm. Cool on the trays. Best served slightly warm. Store in an airtight container for 3–4 days.

Makes 12

Herb Crackers

These crisp cookies can be made in any shape. They are ideal for serving with cheese, or could be crumbled into small pieces and used as croutons for soups and salads.

Preparation time: 25 minutes + 30 chilling
Cooking time: 20–25 minutes

225g self-raising cake flour
1 tsp salt
½ tsp ground white pepper
60g shortening
¾ cup grated hard cheese such as Cheddar or Swiss
3 tbsp freshly chopped parsley
3 tbsp freshly chopped chives

Sift the flour, salt and pepper into a bowl and blend in the shortening. Mix to form a pliable dough by adding 7–8 tablespoons cold water.

On a lightly floured surface, roll the dough into a 38 x 15cm rectangle. Mark lightly into three equal segments. Mix the cheese and herbs together and sprinkle the middle section of pastry with one third of the herbed cheese. Fold up the bottom third, bring the top third down over it, seal the edges and give the pastry a half turn. Repeat the rolling and folding twice more, to use up the herbed cheese. Re-roll and fold once more, then wrap and chill for 30 minutes.

Preheat oven to 180°C (gas mark 4). Lightly grease and flour a baking tray.

Roll out the pastry to a square slightly larger than 30cm. Trim the edges to neaten and then divide into 16 square portions. Transfer to the prepared baking tray and prick all over with a fork. Bake for 20–25 minutes until lightly golden and puffed up. Transfer to a wire rack to cool. Store in an airtight container for up to one week.

Makes 16

Soft Bake Artichoke and Olive Fingers

These luxuriously moist fingers will impress guests at a party or as pre-dinner drinks are served. If preferred, replace the blue cheese with a grated harder cheese such as Cheddar.

Preparation time: 15 minutes
Cooking time: 40–45 minutes

115g plain flour
pinch of salt
85g unsalted butter
¾ cup crumbled blue cheese
⅓ cup tinned artichoke hearts, drained and chopped fine
¼ cup finely chopped pitted black olives
1 egg, beaten
½ tsp paprika

TIP

Once cooled, slip these fingers onto a 18cm cake board and wrap this in aluminium foil to transport safely as a party offering.

Preheat oven to 160°C (gas mark 3). Grease and base-line a 18cm square baking tin.

Sift the flour and salt into a bowl, then blend in the butter until you have fine crumbs. Stir in the cheese, artichokes and olives. Add sufficient egg to bring together to form a dough; reserve the rest of the egg for glazing. Turn onto a lightly floured surface and knead until smooth.

Press the mixture into the prepared tin. Prick all over with a fork and brush lightly with the remaining egg and dust with paprika. Bake in the oven on the middle shelf for 40–5 minutes. Slice in half and then into 12 fingers. Allow to cool in the tin. Store in an airtight container for 3–4 days.

Makes 12

Potato and Chilli Bean Corn Cakes

Little heaps of golden yellow corn with diced potato and kidney beans make these cookies into a substantial snack or an ideal filler or teatime treat.

Preparation time: 10 minutes
Cooking time: 15 minutes

70g cornmeal
55g plain flour
2 tsp baking powder
½ tsp salt
3 tbsp lightly salted butter or
   margarine
¾ cup cubed cooked potato
⅓ cup tinned kidney beans, drained

1 garlic clove, crushed
½ tsp chilli powder
2 tbsp freshly chopped coriander
1 egg, beaten
6 tbsp milk

Preheat oven to 190°C (gas mark 5). Grease or line two baking trays with nonstick baking parchment.

Sift the cornmeal, flour, baking powder and salt into a bowl. Blend the butter or margarine into the dry ingredients until well mixed. Stir in the potato, beans, garlic, chilli powder and coriander. Make a well in the centre and add the egg. Gradually pour in the milk, stirring until the mixture forms a thick batter.

Using a teaspoon, drop 14 heaps, spaced about 5cm apart, onto the prepared baking trays. Bake in the oven for about 15 minutes until lightly golden and firm to the touch. Cool for 10 minutes, then transfer to a wire rack to cool completely. Store in an airtight container for up to five days. Not suitable for freezing.

Makes 14

Index